D

I dedicate this book to all th be okay. It is okay to not be okay. It is right for the feelings to change minute by minute, day by day and month by month. It is okay to laugh and cry, to be sad and angry, to ask questions and to have trust. Have faith that God knows what you need and will provide it. Believe that you are strong. Remember that your track record for surviving bad days is 100%. You've got this!

"For everything there is a season,
a time for every activity under heaven.
A time to be born and a time to die.
A time to plant and a time to harvest.
A time to kill and a time to heal.
A time to tear down and a time to build up.
A time to cry and a time to laugh.
A time to grieve and a time to dance.
A time to scatter stones and a time to gather stones.
A time to embrace and a time to turn away.
A time to search and a time to quit searching.
A time to keep and a time to throw away.
A time to tear and a time to mend.
A time to be quiet and a time to speak.
A time to love and a time to hate.
A time for war and a time for peace."

Ecclesiastes 3:1-8 NLT

Introduction:

Steve and I met in high school and started dating during the end of our junior year. I had never dated anyone else. 'Love of Lifetime' by Firehouse was our song. We were in love, made it through college and got married in 1997. Over the next 9 years, we graduated from college, started teaching careers and had our three boys. We practiced our faith as a family. We put things into place, like life insurance and a will.

Then in 2010, my best friend, Tacy, unexpectedly died at the age of 35. We had a lot of conversations at that point about what we would do if we were in that situation. We only knew that a rule book did not exist.

On Monday, December 18, 2018 Steve had routine hernia surgery. He came home that afternoon and was on the road to recovery. We all went to school on Tuesday morning like a normal day. That afternoon, we learned that he passed away...suddenly, with no warning, but also no pain. His dad, Doug, was with him and held him in his arms. I was in shock. I was in a state of disbelief. How can someone be okay in the morning and gone in the afternoon at 42 years old, a husband, a dad and a teacher? My mother-in-law, Julie, kept saying it wasn't right, he shouldn't go before her.

We were in shock and grief. We went from a family of five to a family of four. I went from being a wife to a widow. My boys suddenly had a single mom for a parent. I thank God for the foundation of faith I had. I told many people that I wasn't sure what I would do if I didn't have my trust in God. I have come to accept that this is God's plan and that we are not in control. I learned through journaling and prayer to be joyful and experience peace.

Everyone and everything tell me that it doesn't matter how long you grieve, that it doesn't end, that it's okay to be upset and struggling. The more grief means the more love. All of this is very true. What no one told me was when it was okay to be okay. When am I allowed to be me and be happy again?

I was strong. I was able to get out of bed most days. I was able to help my boys grieve. I didn't need to feel guilty for smiling and having fun.

Over the past two years, I have learned to be okay, to be able to make it through the day without grief being the main emotion. I have days where I almost forget. I have days where I am not lonely and sad. I have days where I laugh and feel I am moving forward. I have days when I can't hear his voice anymore. I am finding out who I am as a widow, a mom and a woman. I am okay a lot more than not. And it's okay to feel happy, experience joy, and to laugh and smile. It doesn't mean he is forgotten. It doesn't mean the love is gone. It doesn't mean the grief is healed. It just means that I am living the life that God has given me.

My purpose is to share my journey so others can be okay with being okay. God wants you to live here on earth. If He didn't, He would take you home to heaven. It's okay to be okay and yes, also to not be okay...it can change by the minute.

The following is from my journal writings during that first year and a couple during the second year. The scripture is taken from various versions of the Holy Bible. I hope they show how I found Joy through grief and learned that it is truly okay to be okay.

December 20, 2017
The day after Steve went to heaven.

Dear God, I know you have a plan and I am not in control of any of it obviously. I can't make this work. Why Steve? Why did you need him? Why now? Why, when the boys are so young? Why before graduation? Why before we celebrated 25 years, 50 years, 60 years? I know he teased me about being in a relationship for a long time, but it wasn't. Why will I never get another hug or be teased or get to make breakfast anymore? Why? Why? Why? How can I do this alone? How can I be the parent when he's the strong one, the one who got everything? He was the logical part and he loved the boy so much. What do I change? What do I keep the same? How can I learn to make decisions? Do we start eating pork? Can I throw away the cheddar nuggets in the fridge that I bought for him? Can I change the sheets or get rid of his clothes? Can I take down the tree that was his favorite part of Christmas? Can I sell the boat or the truck? Can we make it financially or emotionally? Is my faith strong enough to do this? How do I grieve when I have to take care of everyone else? I have to be a mom. I have to teach. I have to love and give. Where do I look during peace on Sunday? What do I do with the K-Cups in the kitchen? What about Julie? She lost her only son. Does she feel like Mary? What about January? I already made a page for us in my bullet journal with date night. Am I supposed to go on a date by myself? That doesn't make sense. Do I let Matthew sleep with me forever? Do I make a reading corner? Do I move to the guest room? Do I start soon? How long to wait before making changes? How do I have people come for the weekends? How do kids even begin to grasp that you're gone? Why didn't I have any other babies to carry him on? I guess because three is going to be hard with three on my own. He is so loved. What do I do about Christmas? What about life insurance? We didn't get to say goodbye with a hug. Why don't I get to do my bucket list? How do I know what to do about everything? Thank you for unconditionally loving my family, for the funeral home, for Father, for friends, for food. Amen

Strength was my word for the year of 2017. Who knew how much I would need it at the end of the year? God gave me strength all year to be a parent and wife, to stay no to meetings, to say yes to game nights and meals together, and now to endure a funeral and the emptiness. I've been told I'm strong. I'm not sure I've been called that before. God has given me strength. It is a gift.

"And if I go and prepare a place for you,
I will come back and take you to be with me
that you also may be where I am."
John 14:3 NIV

December 29th, 2017

How do I be a single parent? How do I make decisions and know what I'm saying and doing is right for the boys in the long run? Steve was the one that always looked ahead of how things will affect the boys later and how it will make them better more responsible people, workers, spouses, parents, etc. I'm so worried about the boys, Brian especially, I just need to remember that he is an introvert and that it's okay that he can hide out and be himself. I worry about Matthew. He's so little. I hope he has good memories of Steve and knows that he was angry a lot because he was worried a lot of the time, about me, us, the house, his job and the kids at school. I think he also suffered from anxiety and depression (not sleeping, crabby, not liking to be around people) and was affected so much by the winter. He did so much around the house too. I'm so happy he knew enough to set up life insurance and other things so that financially we're going to be okay. I need to get policies like Steve's Prudential for the boys, so they and their families do not worry about general expenses. That's huge. I wonder if I can get something too, so they don't have to worry about me either. I wonder if we should get plots for the boys or let them be with their families if they have them.

"Give justice to the poor and the orphan;
uphold the rights of the oppressed and the
destitute".
Psalm 82:3 NLT

December 30th, 2017

Today I know I can make it through this because of the love and support from everyone but more because of my faith and trust in God. This is his plan. As much as I think it sucks and I'm not sure why it is done, there is nothing any of us can do to make it change or be different. Thank you for giving me 25 years; 42 years for Doug and Julie, 17 years for Michael; 15 years for Brian and 11 years for Matthew. We never know when God will call us home, but I know I will have eternal life with God in heaven. We'll see each other again. Steve is waiting for us. He's with those that have already gone to be our guardian angels.

Are the last six years just borrowed extra bonus time? Should we have lost Steve when the drunk driver crashed into the bedroom? Should we have done so many other things: camp, Washington DC, bobbing with Matthew, going to Hawaii, etc. or was this year at the time already laid out and God's book. I guess this was the time because it happened. I am still in disbelief that I won't see him anymore, no more teasing, hugs and roses, kisses were making love, no more lies about money, no more jokes about my cooking, and no more math tests to grade.

"Just as you cannot understand the path of the wind or the mystery of a tiny baby growing in its mothers' womb, so you cannot understand the activity of God, who does all these things. Plant your seed in the morning and keep busy all afternoon for you don't know if profit will come from one activity or another- or maybe both." Ecclesiastes 11:5-6 NLT

January 1st, 2018

Reflecting on 2017 I think, even with Steve's death, it was a good year. I learned a lot about myself. I increased my faith. I became stronger. I said no to things. I feel more connected to my family. I feel more organized. I feel that I was meant to stay at the middle school. I have so much love and support there, especially now.

"In his kindness God called you to share in his eternal glory by means of Christ Jesus. So, after you have suffered a little while, he will restore, support, and strengthen you, and he will place you on a firm foundation."
1 Peter 5:10 NLT

I don't have the heart to tell Doug that I will be okay and that I have the budget all figured out. I think if we're careful for a while we should be okay with being able to pay off the mortgage, the home equity, the truck, and the Kirkish's credit card. Those amounts are huge. I think we can make it work. It must be. We have no say in any of this. It's all God's plan and so we will work with the gifts he gives us and ask for help when we need it. A friend of mine wrote about how Jesus even asked for help and he was the son of God. Yes, he was in control, but still needed others. He also needed time to be by himself to go off and pray and ask God for what he needed.

"Then Jesus went with them to the olive grove called Gethsemane and he said, "Sit here while I go over there to pray"."
Matthew 26:36

January 3rd, 2018

Yesterday was super frustrating. Why does stuff have to be hard when we're already grieving, not sleeping or eating, and dealing with so much? Why can't there just be a person that contacts you and gives you all the forms you need on one day and you're done. Why is it 15 calls to different places need to be contacted? I'm thankful for the staff at Calumet working to get the sick time paid out. I appreciate Doug for getting me paperwork and phone numbers.

I'm jealous of God who gets to be with him every day anytime He wants. I want that too. I don't just want memories. I want to physically touch him again, to give him a hug and make those tear stains on a shirt. Thank you, God, for the time we had. Thank you for taking him home with you. Thank you for giving us another guardian angel.

"He will wipe every tear from their eyes, and there will be no more death or sorrow or crying or pain. All these things are gone forever." Revelations 21:4

Home today. My brain tells me to take a day, my heart tells me I need to teach, or the other way around. The boys are all taking a day too. Maybe we'll need to do this for a while. Matthew is very attached to me. I was the only one that could drop him off and pick him up from the basketball last night. He's still sleeping with me in my room downstairs. He doesn't want to go upstairs to his room, which is totally understandable with the loss of his dad. I'm sure he's worried I'm going to die too. I really hope that God doesn't need me now for everyone's sake. Not sure anyone could survive that right now. The kids are asking me at school about staying as Mrs. Lancour. I never even thought about changing my name and I don't think I will. I still feel married to Steve. I can't imagine taking my ring off, let alone changing my name.

Fatty liver infiltration. Wow! Who knew? It was God's plan no matter what. I guess it just would've been nice to know and see if there's anything we could have done or known.

I signed up for meals to be delivered. It's really hard to ask for help, that's for sure. I think it's good to let others help. Mary accepted comfort at the foot of the cross. Jesus accepted help and he prayed a lot to God about his life, wants, dreams, etc.

"Abba, Father", he cried out, "everything is possible for you. Please take this cup of suffering away from me. Yet I want your will to be done, not mine."
Mark 14:36 NLT

January 6th, 2018

Matthew was so attached, confused, angry and I think just plain missing Steve. Missing his comments, his teasing, his routines with Matthew (don't sit on your sandwich). Does anyone know if he said that on Tuesday? It breaks my heart to see all three of them grieving. I have to remember that my family is grieving too. They're not just here to help me with the boys. They lost a son and a brother. I need to keep that in my brain. I need to ask how they are and what they need. Matt checks on us all daily, but who's checking on him. I feel selfish not realizing the grief they feel too. They are all trying to be parents and be strong for me and the boys. Maybe people need to go to a grief counselor. I need someone to tell me that my acceptance is normal this soon. I have put it all to God and know that it's always and forever according to his plan.

"Where have you put him?", he asked them.
They told him, "Lord, come and see."
Then Jesus wept.
The people who were standing nearby said,
"See how much he loved him!".
John 11:34-36 NLT

My heart is breaking more. Matthew finally talked a little last night. He told me, "You don't understand what I'm going through" and I told him I do. I know he's scared that he's going to lose me too and that he really misses Steve, but I also told them that I'm grieving because I lost my best friend. I wish we could all grieve in the same way on the same day at the same time so we're all in tears, or all angry or all need quiet and cuddles or share memories and laugh. But I know that can't happen. I also want someone to be able to tell me when it's time to clean up or get rid of the shampoo in the shower and what's right for us all. So that by leaving things some of us are not upset and yet moving stuff affects another person. Sometimes I wish I could just shut my brain off so I wouldn't have to worry so much about the boys. I hope we can all grieve a little more, have some hard conversations to start to heal and find a new normal.

God,
I know this is all part of your plan and I know you never give more than we can handle but please guide me through the grief and love and coping. Grant me peace in my days. Guide me of what to say and do, not only for myself, but for the boys in the family, for every one that loved him. I want to be selfish and take all the attention while at the same time I know that everyone else needs to grieve as well. Let me know when to cry with others. Let me know if I'm trying to be too strong.
Amen

"I have told you these things, so that in me you may have peace. In this world you will have trouble. But take heart! I have overcome the world."
John 16:33 NIV

I'm just upset that I'm not going to be strong enough to support the boys and get them through my own grieving as well. I worry about breaking down in front of them even though I know it's good for them to see others' grief. I think others are doing the same thing; not being upset when they are around me or the boys. We all get it. Even Matthew gets it.

"But if it were me, I would encourage you. I would try to take away your grief."
Job 16:5 NLT

Steve would say I'm stressed because I'm filling my calendar, but I think grief and stress are a lot alike and I need to be busy to keep my mind going and not just focus on the loss. I think by doing things like yoga and painting that it's more self-care than avoidance. I need to contact people to set up appointments for counseling. None of the boys are ready to see anyone yet. I texted them so it'd be more permanent that if something happened, they could go back and read the text from me. It was good to look at messages on Steve's phone the other day. I guess I should change the answering machine message too so that it's not Steve's voice. I also need to update my phone with the in case of emergency contact info to be my parents and remove it from Steve's name.

I need everyone to pick up an article of clothing for the bear or fish that Kendra is going to have made. Even if they don't want it now, they might at some point, like the stuff that Julie is collecting for them to have it another point in their lives, like death certificates, photos and the obituary. I wonder if she wants his birth certificate or marriage license to go with those things. I'll have to ask. I need to make sure I keep writing poetry and doing journaling. It's what I'm doing to take care of myself and I think it's helpful. Sundays still suck with the memories of us going to church every week and having conversations about the boy or work or whatever, being at church together, having lunch as a family and just hanging out at home. It's so weird. It's still not real. Why is he not in the bathroom getting ready to start his day? Why do I have to be alone?

I wish my sister could move back here to the area. She leaves tomorrow and it's going to be weird. But I guess that's part of the adjustment to a new normal. I still can't believe he's gone. It still doesn't seem real. He should be in bed right now getting ready to go and teach. I should be making coffee, his lunch and wrapping a breakfast sandwich. He should get up and shut the door. He should tease me about something. He should complain about the stupid crazy Wednesday schedule. He should be here. He should still be listening to music and turning on the radio three minutes before he leaves in the morning. He should tell the boys to get up and how much he loves them. He should tell Matthew not to sit on his sandwich. He should buy me flowers when I have a bad day. He should rub my back for two seconds with one finger when I asked for a back rub. He should let me cry on his shoulder and make tear stains on a shirt. He should be here. He should not be gone. This sucks and it's still unbelievable.

"My heart is filled with bitter sorrow and unending grief"
Romans 9:2 NLT

I miss you so much. I don't want you to be gone. I don't want this to be true. I can't understand why you didn't get to be here anymore. I know I was overtired last night, and I am grieving and that I was alone but now it really hurts. My heart is broken. I'm being strong. My faith, our faith, is getting me through. My friends and family support are such a comfort. I love how we can all be together.

I wonder if I'd gone first, would you make changes? Would you move? Would you get remarried.? You didn't have any answers when Tacy died and I guess you wouldn't have them now either. There are no rules, no rights or wrongs, and no time guidelines of what to do when to do what. It's hard to believe you're gone. It must be a nightmare that I can't wake up from. Hard to see the blessings and good in this whole thing. I know you see me and are probably thinking I should go back to bed instead of journaling but has always and forever been my thing. I love you. I miss you. I'm jealous of you being in heaven with everyone else I've lost. I'm glad you're watching over all of us. I'm so happy you had such a strong faith, so much love, and such an amazing sense of humor. Keep watching me, the boys, your parents, my family and your school crew.

"Though he brings grief, he also shows compassion because of the greatness of his unfailing love." Lamentations 3:32 NLT

January 13th, 2018

Tomorrow is the anniversary of Bruce dying and then 2 weeks till Tacy. A month between Steve, Blanche, Bruce and Tacy. I miss them all. So glad I still get signs from them often to let me know they are in heaven with God, our ultimate goal in life.

I have a phone call to a therapist. I'm excited to talk with her. I'm hoping that once a month with her will be enough or if I'm going to need to find someone else. I wonder if I should see a grief counselor. Someone that has that area of specialty. I wonder when to take down the Christmas tree and how hard it will be to put away his ornaments. Once the boys are gone from home, the plan is to use his, mine and ours. I guess that is not something I need to decide right now. I worry about being here by myself after Matthew leaves for college. Again, something a long way down the road, but I'm worried. I hate being home alone for a few hours, and not at night for sure. Or any length of time like days and weeks. I hope the kids get married and they choose to live in this area, and I can have a relationship like them with I had with my grandparents and Steve did with his and the boys do now.

I can't wait for the beach to be clear of snow. I feel so close to you, and God when I'm near the water.

"The Lord will guide you continually, giving you water when you are dry and restoring your strength. You will be like a well-watered garden, like an ever-flowing spring."
Isaiah 58:11 NLT

January 14th, 2018

'Right here waiting for you.' I'm so happy to know you're in heaven. 'Oceans apart.' Waiting for me. 'I can hear you, but it doesn't stop the pain'. I want to be able to talk to you. I want to be near you. My heart is so broken and there's so much to do and I don't want to be responsible. I can't hear you now. 'Whatever you do I will be right here waiting for you.'

Stacy asked yesterday if you come to visit and if it's hard for you. I've always believed in heaven there is no pain so I guess it doesn't hurt you do it because you still love us and always will. I love knowing you can still see me. I hope we're doing okay and that we make you proud. I hope you're able to laugh and smile at us. I want you to know that I don't see myself ever getting remarried. I am forever yours faithfully. I don't want anyone else to kiss me. Maybe today I can sort through the box of all our letters to remove the personal ones so that the kids can read the others. I pray our marriage is an example for them. I hope Matthew has enough memories to grow up with to be able to live a life like we had: Commitment. Love. Faithfulness. Honor. Being there for each other through everything, no matter how hard.

I know you still love me, but I want to hear it again. I want to feel you hug me, to rub my thumb during church, to squeeze too hard during peace, to rub your knee while we pray, or to rub your back or feet. I'm so glad I was able to help your shoulder a little bit and that you're no longer in pain now. Do you feel young? You were feeling so old and you weren't that old.

Why God? I don't know why you think I can do this without the love of my life here. How do I be a single parent? It doesn't seem right. How do I make decisions on my own? I know I can ask you for guidance. I know you have Steve watching over me, but this is just so hard. I hate grief. I hate being sad. I want to accept your plan and to be confident that I've got this, that I'll be okay, that the boys will be okay and that his legacy was long enough for him to live forever in the boys. That they'll be able to use our marriage and parenting to have a great marriage and love being a couple and parents as much as Steve and I did. I want their faith to grow in this. I want them to be okay. I want them to pray, to cry, to talk it out. I want them to grieve around me. I want everyone to not feel that they have to hide their tears if I'm not crying. I want to be able to ask for and accept help, a strength I've always listed for the kids at school.

"No one has ever seen God. But if we love each other, God lives in us, and his love is brought to full expression in us."
1 John 4:12 NLT

January 15th, 2018

Today I learned about STUG (sudden temporary uprising of grief). The weird things that make grief real again without any rational explanation. Not that anything is rational, it's all according to God.

"For I am always aware of your unfailing love, and I have lived according to your truth."
Psalm 26:3 NLT

January 16th, 2018

One month. Too hard to believe. Too hard to comprehend. Four weeks without you and I've made it. I don't know if I'm doing a good job or not but we're all sleeping and eating and going to school and other events, so I guess we're okay. I had to visit Matt last night. He misses you so much too. I hate being a burden on others that are grieving but I guess I just needed a hug. Why are you not here? Why do I have to be alone? Why can't you come back and be with me? Why can't you help me make decisions?

I got the life insurance check today. Thank you for having everything set up so we'll be okay. What's with the leak roofing? Just so we have something to do? Things to fix like you always had to do. I have so much to do and no desire to do any of it. Not to do paperwork, taxes, FAFSA, progress reports, grades, nothing. Why do they stick in my head so much? The last 6 weeks suck. I'm sorry I have not made the boys study for exams. I'm sorry I never kept up on Spanish. I'm sorry if I'm doing this wrong with the boys, your family, my family, the paperwork, school and work, the relationships. It's just too much to decide. I hate making decisions. What if I'm making them wrong and people get hurt?

"Wise choices will watch over you.
Understanding will keep you safe."
Proverbs 2:11 NLT

January 17th, 2018

I'm so thankful for our boys being big enough and old enough to make a meal or take showers and do homework, independently. I hope I haven't been too lenient with them, but this grief piece thoroughly sucks. I feel it's sucking my brain and draining my energy. I need to sleep and not have to think. There have been more blessings than there are worries in this situation. God took Steve home with Him because it was his time, but only because He knew it was set before everyone else. Someday, hopefully after the boys are grown and have kids and are in a space that they can cope. I don't think now is the time to make many changes especially with Matthew; he's so little. I can't imagine dealing with losing your dad. I can't imagine it now and I'm 42 and I don't see him every day we're still learning from him constantly. I do learn from him and love him and need support, but not in a way that you do when you're 11, 15 or 17. Still too much to understand and death, grieving and loss, to feel weak, will make a strong. Without stress we break. We need to take what we've learned and grow from it. We need to accept without question or confusion.

"You have endowed him with eternal blessings and given him the joy of your presence."
Psalm 21:6 NLT

January 18th, 2018

I hope I'm not sharing too much with Michael about the budget, but I don't ever want him to be where we were before with a ton of debt and no way to pay it off without drastic measures. I'm so glad Steve knew and understood budgeting. I love to do it and I'm irritated that I can't redo my budget until March once I know about social security and retirement, etc. I think I'm going to start with a new notebook knowing I can rip out pages or use binder clips for those or something. I think having it, even for two months is better than not having it done and looking at the post-its and notes with Steve's name. I also need to figure out the credit card at some point.

I'm still angry and a little confused about why Steve had to go now. Why when you, God, make plans, why can't you share a little more with us ahead of time or give us a little more about the why or give us a sign of some sort? Why do we always have to wonder when I will go? When will someone go? What if we're not the way we should be? What if I'm making all the wrong decisions for me for the boys and for the kids at school?

I have learned a few things. I am strong. I am enough. I am lovable. I am loved. I am smart. I am kind. I'm able to be on my own. I am a great mom. I am good at writing, photography, prayer, organization and budgeting.

"On the first day of each week, you should each put aside a portion of the money you have earned. Don't wait until I get there and then try to collect it all at once."
1 Corinthians 16:2 NLT

January 19th, 2018

Help me continue accepting Steve being gone and go through the grief process and be able to make the right decisions about moving his stuff around or getting rid of his stuff or making donations of his clothes. Help me go through his files and know what to keep and what not to save. Help me decide what to do about going to North Carolina over spring break. Am I okay? Am I doing what's right? I know that, Steve, you're not mad at me for not putting my foot down and being strong and doing or saying what I think you would do. I'm sorry I always made you the bad guy when it came to decision-making all along. Thank you for forcing me to make decisions. I guess you knew, and God knew that I would need it. Sometimes I will have to be the bad guy, but for now there are no rules. We said that when Tacy died. No one knows what is right. I feel we raise good boys who see us as an example because we gave them love, discipline and faith. We've had high expectations for them as far as academics, doing chores and attending church. I hope they can look at the memories and remember what we both have told them all along. God knows what we need to happen. As much as losing my friend sucked and was shocking and unbelievable, maybe 2010 was all just prep for 2017. We all have grieved, and we all know we can survive, life goes on, time helps heal, we are loved and supported. We are examples for others to follow and I can be strong, a leader and it will be okay.

"God uses it to prepare and equip his people to do every good work." 2 Timothy 3:17 NLT

January 20th, 2018

I love being able to still text you but I'm not sure who is ever going to be able to read them.

I'm not sure I should have read some of the texts he got but I'm glad I did. I'm so glad Steve was here long enough to save Matt, to see my relationships with coworkers change, to help me raise the boys and to get things started on the school board. Oh, he's going to be so missed in so many places: the MEA, the school board, church, the middle school, and home. Especially home. I think others will move on and get new people.

I don't see me moving on in that way and getting a new person and being able to share my house or give my body or my heart with another man. A heart could grow a new space, there's no limit to that but I'm not sure my soul or emotions are ready for that. I'm okay being alone, being a single parent, a friend, etc without Steve or anybody else.

"My health may fail, and my spirit may grow weak, but God remains the strength of my heart; he is mine forever."
Psalm 23:76 NLT

January 21st, 2018

I wish I could still get a hug from you and no one else is right
or a good enough substitute.

I know my faith is why I'm as okay as I am. I know God is
watching over me. I want Him to be happy with how I'm
doing. I want Him to guide me through my life and allow me to
see His works in the connection with Jesus, his only son, and in
the Holy Spirit who helps me or causes me to make decisions. I
want to be at peace so it's visible to everyone I meet and work
with.

"For the Holy Spirit will teach you
at that time what needs to be said."
Luke 12:12 NLT

January 23rd, 2018

Thank you, God, for time to sleep last night and for everything to get done. I'm not sure. I want to be busy. I want to do self-care. I want to be with people, but I also know I need to make sure it's not causing more stress to try to be at something every day.

I feel a little guilty about taking a sick day, but Brian asked me and sometimes a break is good. I'm going to get something done for Steve's estate too. It's weird to call it that, but I guess it's better than funeral stuff since that was really only two days.

I miss you so much. I love you. I love the memories we shared.

"The younger son told his father, 'I want my share of your estate now before you die.' So, his father agreed to divide his wealth between his sons."
Luke 15:12 NLT

January 25th, 2018

I hate to be alone. How am I going to do this once Matthew leaves? Can I be okay in the house? Which is why we had enough to pay it off so that if I or the kids needed, we could move. Right now, I need to live here. I need the memories, the projects, our room, his stuff. I also need to take some time to sort our box with all the journals, cards, letters etc. that we sent to each other, mostly while we were dating. I need to read it and remove the really personal stuff but leave the rest for my boys, our grandkids or great grandkids if they want to read them to see what the letters look like since everyone does technology now.

I hope Steve knows that my mom worried about him when he snowblowed and wishes she had said she loved him more when he was alive. I'm not sure I have a lot of regrets. Steve knew I loved him and that I was the love of his lifetime. I still assume he's mine too. It still sucks to have to pay off the home equity and mortgage which is something we wanted to do together and not sure we'd ever pay the mortgage off, but plan was to live here forever anyway so it didn't matter. Maybe it's a blessing and I know it's all part of God's plan. It's meant to be the way it is but it's not easy. It sucks. I would pay that forever if I could have Steve here to pay it with me. I love you and I miss you.

"They are brand new, not things from the past. So, you cannot say, 'We knew that all the time!'" Isaiah 48:7 NLT

January 28th, 2018

I want to see someone. It took me six weeks to see somebody when Tacy died and it's been almost that long that Steve died. A friend recommended someone at the hospital, which is easy since it's across the street.

I'm so happy that Brian helped me with the annoying project of piecing together all the love songs that I mushed together into one track.

It's so weird how neither of us really changed since the engaged encounter. He still tried to fix everything, and I still cry and write more than talk even though I talk a lot and interrupt. I guess since we got together and we're that way, that's why it worked for us. I can't believe he's gone way too soon. What happened to us making it to 50 or 70 years of marriage? I'm not sure I can count more years even though I feel we are still married, and I don't want to be with anyone else.

"For the Christian wife brings holiness to her marriage, and the Christian husband brings holiness to his marriage. Otherwise, your children would not be holy, but now they are holy." 1 Corinthians 7:14

January 29th, 2018

I'm back to crying like in high school, like in college, like 4 years ago, and with Tacy 8 years ago. Maybe I can only hold it together for 4 years. I do plan to see a counselor and I think the boys should also. Do we need referrals if we just make appointments?

I'm supposed to go and pay the mortgage off tomorrow. Why do I struggle so much when it should be a happy thing?

I am glad I keep my old journals and letters and that Steve saved too. It's been fun to go through them all.

"And the Spirit of the Lord will rest on him—
the Spirit of wisdom and understanding,
the Spirit of counsel and might, the Spirit of
knowledge and the fear of the Lord."
Isaiah 11:2 NLT

January 30th, 2018

I'm hoping the counselor will be able to connect with me and me with her; to be able to offer comfort and advice. I hope she has a strong faith. My last counselor was able to connect my therapy to faith and that was helpful. I know if I'm not comfortable that I can try someone else and I can find a good fit or match.

Subconsciously, I think Tuesdays are hard because that's the day Steve died. Maybe today is going to be better.

"Let the message about Christ, in all its richness, fill your lives. Teach and counsel each other with all the wisdom he gives. Sing psalms and hymns and spiritual songs to God with thankful hearts."
Colossians 3:16 NLT

Made it through six weeks. Paid off the mortgage. Didn't have a huge gain at Weight Watchers. Talked to my doctor, who did the referral to see a counselor. She is supposed to be great.

Feeling tired today but ready for meditation tonight. I think it's interesting how much I have not changed since high school as far as my crying journaling and seeing someone. I guess this is just my life. I need to remember to do journaling and letter writing or poetry or something since that's always been my go-to for coping. I'd like to get together with others too that have lost people. We need a support group for widows. I hate that word. It sounds icky. Not sure what would be good: spouseless, alone, abandoned, separate? I'm not sure, but not the word widow.

I need to figure out how to sleep, to do homework, to do self-care, to eat, and to clean the house. I need some balance and success in this house. I need to make the boys step up and start cleaning and doing dishes again to help out. I can't do it all. I do need help.

"But in my distress, I cried out to the LORD; yes, I cried to my God for help. He heard me from his sanctuary; my cry reached his ears."
2 Samuel 22:7 NLT

February 5th, 2018

I've been seeing a counselor this week and hopefully that can help me make some decisions and validate my thoughts and feelings.

I had a hard time at church yesterday. I don't know how to answer the question, "what do you need"? I don't know if I need anything. Am I supposed to need something? Am I doing too much on my own? Am I not doing something that I should be? Should I need help? Is it because I'm not good at asking for help and so I'm not? Is it because I struggle with making decisions and the question is open-ended enough to be a decision? I don't feel I need anything. I feel I have enough with my close friends and family and my faith is my rock. I have an appointment to see someone. I've talked with the boys. I guess I'd like to know if they need something, but they aren't letting me know. It was hard to be crying in church, and I know it was bothering Matthew, but he needs to see me grieve too.

"O people of Zion, who live in Jerusalem, you will weep no more. He will be gracious if you ask for help. He will surely respond to the sound of your cries." Isaiah 30:19 NLT

February 6th, 2018

I need to walk today. I need to pray the rosary. I need to meditate. I need to sleep. I need some time on my own. Everybody needs some time all alone and I've not had that since Steve died. 7 weeks ago, today. Maybe that's it. Tuesday is not my day because of that. Maybe it's in my brain somewhere and I didn't even know it.

"He was alone at the time because his disciples had gone into the village to buy some food." John 4:8 NLT

February 7th, 2018

I am struggling. Am I doing okay as a mom? Am I doing okay as a teacher? Am I doing okay with grief? Am I doing too much to try to cope? Am I strong enough when I need to be? Am I strong enough to be in my new normal?

"But when they measured it out, everyone had just enough. Those who gathered a lot had nothing left over, and those who gathered only a little had enough. Each family had just what it needed." Exodus 16:18 NLT

Last night was awful. I just sobbed. Couldn't stop. Didn't want to. The boys tried to comfort me, and it didn't work. I didn't want them to feel they needed to and maybe it's good to be taken care of, but I wanted Steve to be here and hug me so bad. I miss the physical touch so much. I just want a hug.

This is the new part of grief that I didn't know existed. I know the confusion, the numbness, the loss, the left behind, the anger, the hurt, the wanting to call, God's plan, the loneliness, the new normal, that life goes on, and to take it one more day at a time. All those pieces from losing Tacy, Grandma and Grandpa, Blanche, Bruce and grandparents, etc. I thought I'd be okay. I thought I could do this. I've been strong. I've had faith that this is how it's meant to be. I cried. I've hurt. I've been lonely. I wrote journals. I prayed. I've talked. I've seen a counselor. I've been up all night. I've slept. I'd eaten without knowing it. I've been done but this is all so different.

The paperwork, the logistics, the new role as a single parent, stuff at work, the guilt of sharing with others, the unknowing of what I need, feeling of knowing I need Steve, and no one can give me that.

I joked with him on that Sunday about having the life insurance all set and Steve didn't find it funny. He knew he was dying. He knew it. He felt old. He was hurting. He did things with the boys. He took Brian to the movies. He had Michael do all the insulation projects. He shopped alone with Matthew. I don't know what we did. What was my moment that I should have seen? I don't know. I don't think we had anything that we didn't normally have. We were having monthly date nights, still parenting, we went for rides to talk, we prayed at church together, we laughed, we loved, but deep down I think he knew.

 He was so scared of the surgery, so nervous something would get punctured or damaged or leak. Did he know about his liver? How come we didn't see it? Why was it so quick? I'm glad he didn't have to suffer at all, his knee and shoulder were enough. He wasn't himself. He played Monopoly with us and Skylar. He got everything for Christmas. He gave up buildings and grounds committee and coaching Lego League. We talked about not camping. We talked about graduation. We talked about the bathroom and drywall. He had all the insurance and retirement figure it out. He knew what he wanted. I don't wish for it to have been me. I don't know if I'm ready. I know it's not my decision, but maybe because I do finances, the cleaning, the grocery shopping, taxes, etc. that God knew I could do this because grief is pretty much the only new thing. I think God knows that I've got this. "Don't worry," says God. Mary was able to carry and raise the king of the world, our Savior, and I know she was scared. I do got this!

"But Mary kept all these things in her heart
and thought about them often."
Luke 2:19 NLT

February 11th, 2018

I'm so thankful for all the time we had together. My Facebook post from 8 years ago talked about us meeting in sixth grade, dating in 1992 and getting married in 1997. I still thought we'd get to 50 years of marriage or longer. I wish I had known that when you said you were feeling so old that it meant you were going to be gone. I don't want to be here without you. We've never been apart this long in 25 years. I miss you.

I have peace knowing you'll always be in my heart. I have peace knowing you're watching over me now. I have peace knowing you'll guide the boys forever. I have peace knowing God needed you more. I have peace knowing I'll be with you again. I have peace remembering our years together. I have peace sharing memories of you and us. I have peace.

"Truly my soul finds rest in God;
my salvation comes from him."
Psalm 62:1 NIV

February 12th, 2018

"Perfect" is the new Ed Sheeran song. I can hear it coming from Steve. 'Dancing in the dark with you between my arms, you are perfect tonight.'

I need some time to be me, to clean, to decide about Steve's stuff, to read grief books, to go out to lunch with friends, to meditate, to do yoga, to walk, work on my Bible study, to sleep and be here more for the boys that I have been, to work on my journals, to make ornaments and photo albums, to organize our love letters and wedding stuff, and to finalize the paperwork and the budget. I think the next two weeks off is what I need. I need someone to do my job for me for the next little bit. I need to be me, to be a mom, a wife, meditator, Bible study facilitator, and a friend. I need to take care of myself, so I can take care of others.

"Cast all your anxiety on him because he cares for you. "1 Peter 5:7 NIV

2 months. The longest by far that we've ever been apart. The longest without a phone call or letter, hugs or kisses. Even when we first started dating, it wasn't this long. I sure miss seeing you, holding you, laughing with you, and being romantic. I don't know why I'm here without you. I know it's God's plan for me to be without you, but I don't see why. To be a widow and a wife, a single mom and a parent. I know this whole situation is making me stronger, but I was okay being weak. Being dependent on you, on our relationship, on the fact that we could decide things, we could talk and fight and disagree, we could do what we thought was best. I guess I still can say 'we', but I know I'm relying on conversations we had, discussions about everything. I just want to know that I'm doing okay and I'm making the best decisions for me and for the boys. I hate that everyone else is grieving too. Maybe if it were only me, I'd be okay to talk and cry. Maybe everyone would know what to do. Maybe everything would be fine and not awkward and hard like it is now. I want everyone to be okay at our house. I want to be okay with your mom and dad's. I want them to be okay. Thank you for visiting your sister. Thank you for visiting me. I wish I could feel you. I miss getting a hug with you with my arms all tucked in and you squishing me and letting me cry for a while before you make a joke or tease me about something.

"Trust in the Lord with all your heart
and lean not on your own understanding"
Proverbs 3:5 NIV

I feel a little lost today not celebrating Valentine's Day, not that we would have gone out tonight anyway, too crowded at restaurants. I organized some pictures that I made into photo albums for the boys and me. Part of me is ready to be home alone and part of me is okay with someone else being here too.

I love my boys so much and I really wish I could take away the pain for them. I know through suffering we grow stronger. Father Ben's sermon was so perfect Monday night. He talked about not seeking suffering, but when it comes to persevere and grow because of it. I feel that way. Is this to make me a better mom, a better me, to help others to learn more about resurrection and heaven in my feelings?

My therapist validated me. She's proud of how I'm healing and to allow others to grieve to and recognize that. I needed the recognition and validation that I'm doing okay.

"Not only so, but we also glory in our sufferings because we know that suffering produces perseverance; perseverance, character, and character, hope."
Romans 5:3-4 NIV

February 16th, 2018

No heat and you're not here to take care of it. Michael helped. It's working now but I want you to swear and go to the basement. What am I going to do when all the boys leave home? Can I be here alone? Do I want to stay? Right now, I do. I think the boys do too, although maybe it should be a conversation.

I love the life we shared for 25 years. I love how we shared all parts of our lives and how faithful we both were always. I don't feel we had any really serious arguments. I did walk out, but I think that was my messed-up brain not you or us or our relationship.

"A woman is bound to her husband as long as he lives. But if her husband dies, she is free to marry anyone she wishes, but he must belong to the Lord. In my judgment, she is happier if she stays as she is— and I think that I too have the Spirit of God."
1 Corinthians 7:39-40

February 18th, 2018

Steve always wanted the boys to be responsible, respectful, smart, and loving. He always asked me when we had conversations if I wanted them to be dependent on us. I still don't. I want them to know how to clean a house and have ethics to work hard and be proud of themselves. I hope our parenting style taught them those values. I hope our marriage is an example to them about how to live and love. I hope they can each find someone as special as Steve was to me; someone to talk with; laugh with; be faithful: have discussions; have faith; and be the love of their lifetime.

"However, each one of you also must love his wife as he loves himself, and the wife must respect her husband." Ephesians 5: 33 NIV

February 23rd, 2018

Thank you, God, for giving me time off to think and to rework my goals for my career. I think I've got control of my grief as much as I can. It's not easy and it still sucks that Steve is gone. It's still not real most of the time but I know I'll get through. When you get replanted by God, like a real tree, it takes a while to adjust to the new soil, but then I'll flourish and grow in my new place. I think God has repotted me.

"He took one of the seedlings of the land and put it in fertile soil. He planted it like a willow by abundant water, and it sprouted and became a low, spreading vine. Its branches turned toward him, but its roots remained under it. So, it became a vine and produced branches and put out leafy boughs".
Ezekiel 17:5-6 NIV

February 24th, 2018

Self-care Day Two: journal, pray, walk, yoga, Mass, soup, family, read, a game, no paperwork, no errands, no rushing around: just be today. Be still and know that I am God. If only we could chuck a pumpkin at death and destroy it, but really, we all want to die to be with God, to be in heaven. It's part of the promise. Death is the only guarantee we have. We don't even know why or when or how, but we know what's going to happen. There is nothing we can do to stop it, nothing to change even when it's going to happen.

Live as if you were going to die tomorrow. Love is if today is the last day you've got. Be with others because tomorrow they may be gone. Talk to others and share memories and make new ones. God knows he's taking us home and keeps it a secret. We all know death is the only thing we know for sure. Deep down we all want to die to be with God. Our greatest desire needs to be getting to heaven. Doing all that we can with the time we have in case God's plan comes true. No one knows the hour of our journey to heaven starts. No one knows when it's our turn to join family and friends. God put us here for a specific length of time long enough for his purpose. God controls everything and we need to be okay with that or we'll be miserable for earthly lifetime.

God knows. Why doesn't he share? God knows. Why can't I know too? God knows. Give control to him. God knows. He takes us when it's time. God knows. I think we'll know a little too. God knows.

"But about that day or hour no one knows, not even the angels in heaven, nor the Son, but only the Father." Matthew 24:36 NIV

February 27th, 2018

Steve always said we should be okay financially, but I'd still have to work. He knew he was going to die before we retired. He always seemed to know what we needed with the mortgage and knowing I'd have to still work. I wonder what signs God gave him to be so ready. He showed his love to everyone. He was stepping back from things like buildings and grounds committee at church and Lego at school. He was thankful football was over. He went to the movies with Brian. He took Matthew shopping. He finished the insulation project with Michael. He got the carpeting knowing we needed it to finish the space. He didn't ask about finances as much this fall. He made all the improvements on the house but never set up the appraisal. We never shifted our investments to another person. He had the gifts for me for Christmas. We talked about selling the camper. We looked at college or no college for Michael. And everything was so set up.

My faith over the last 3 months has grown so much. I know I needed it for Bruce's death and now for this time. I wish my faith could help Matthew more. I wish I could pray his grief away. I wish I could get him to feel safe enough to go to school. I wish I knew what to say and what to do. Sometimes we just need to lay in bed and cry. Sometimes school, and food and being awake is just too much.

God,

Thank you for my strength. I know it comes from you. Please guide me as the best way to serve Matthew, Michael, and Brian. Amen.

"Therefore, keep watch because you do not know when the owner of the house will come back—whether in the evening, or at midnight, or when the rooster crows, or at dawn."
Mark 32:35 NIV

February 28th, 2018

Beautiful trauma. That's what Steve being gone without warning is.

God's will was brought up yesterday during counseling. I've never really thought about it other than that I don't think many of my students have the faith piece in their lives so it's hard for them to cope or understand God's plan if you don't believe or worship or praise and petition him on a daily basis. I don't know why God doesn't step in and make changes. And I do, it's called free will. God lets us choose. Through him we have the strength to make good choices and defeat Satan's plan. I know God is the strongest. He defeats death, but I also know he doesn't control us when we don't let him into our lives. We need God to guide us, protect us, love us, and take us home to heaven to live with him there when our time is done here. Maybe I haven't done enough of my purpose yet. Maybe there's more with the kids at school, or my own boys, or the orphanage that needs to be dealt with and in only way I can do. I don't know and I don't understand the plan written down for us, but I believe what happens, happens for a reason and it's already determined for us as long as we choose God in our faith. God will continue to guide me to him according to his plan and I can only deviate if I choose to ignore my heart, my faith and God's love for me. God won't let us suffer as long as we believe it.

"Trust in the Lord with all your heart
and lean not on your own understanding"
Proverbs 3:5 NIV

Not sure I'm doing okay as a parent right now. All three boys are home. I don't know what to say to the boys. I can't make the grief go away. I can't guarantee that everything is going to stay as it is now or that I'm going to be alive for a long time. It's really hard to have that much faith and mine didn't come overnight. Mine has come through a lot of grief, trauma, miracles, survival and experiences. I pray that God works through them and shows them all they are capable of.

Dear Lord God,
Please be with my boys. Teach them your love Grace and peace, show them the miracles of the holy spirit so their faith is increased and they find strength to begin a new normal that includes going to school being with friends, attending Mass, prayer, gratitude, being friendly, continuing successes with academics, laughing and crying, sharing memories and breathing while living at the same time. Help them sleep. Help them dream about you and get to be with you and Steve again someday in heaven. Show them how to live so they can be the best version of themselves and fulfill the purpose you have for them. Let them see the 'why' behind Steve's death. Let them know that it's okay that you've got this, and you won't let them drown in the storm that they are in the middle of right now. Help the waves slow and stop crashing so hard. Help them smile and remember Steve's love for them and the hopes and dreams we share for them. Guide them to you. Amen.

"The disciples went and woke him, saying, "Master, Master, we're going to drown!" He got up and rebuked the wind and the raging waters. The storm subsided, and all was calm." Luke 8:24 NIV

March 9th, 2018

I sure miss you. I am still struggling with you being gone. On one hand seems like you've been gone so long and yet it's only been nine or ten weeks. January and February seemed really long and it's hard to believe it's already March 9th. I wish you were here to offer your opinion on the whole situation. I need to turn my worries and stress over to God.

"Do not be anxious about anything, but in every situation, by prayer and petition, with thanksgiving, present your requests to God. And the peace of God, which transcends all understanding, will guard your hearts and your minds in Christ Jesus."
Philippians 4:6-7 NIV

March 13th, 2018

Steve why aren't you here to help me out? You always know what to say, especially in situations like this. Thank you for wanting to talk with people back in November with me. I love you.

Dear Lord,

Give me continued strength to go to work and to teach, my passion. Help me focus on the kids and not the situation. I turn it over to you to do with as you see fit. Amen.

"He will cover you with his feathers, and under his wings you will find refuge; his faithfulness will be your shield and rampart."
Psalm 91:4 NIV

March 19th, 2018

God,

Please guide me. Continue to open doors. Help me learn what I need to do. Help me know what decision to make. Help me be smart, not just excited. Continue to love me and give me strength. Amen.

"Direct me in the path of your commands,
for there I find delight."
Psalm 119:35 NIV

Yesterday during prayer, I had a very cool experience. I was on a bridge. I have the choice to live in the past with those that have died or move forward and choose God. I can always decide but God can take my burdens away and give me rest.

"Praise be to the Lord, to God our Savior,
who daily bears our burdens."
Psalm 68:19 NIV

March 22nd, 2018

After break I need to be stronger and make them go to school like you would have. I miss you so much, your hugs, your teasing, your smile, your advice, your kindness, your strength, your love. I wish you didn't have to go. I wish God had left you here a little longer. You'd tell me I was a good mom and a good teacher. You tell me that I'll be okay. I've got this. You prepared me for 25 years to be able to do this. You gave the boys enough while you were here, and I know you're still watching over us every day. I'm sorry I'm not making them go, even though I know if the situation were reversed, I think you'll make them go. Would it be harder on everyone? It would be very different, you getting everyone up, breakfast with Matthew, routines, meals together. I think you'd be dealing with it better than me. I love you. I miss you. It sucks without you. It's hard without you. I don't like it without you.

"Whether you turn to the right or to the left, your ears will hear a voice behind you, saying, 'This is the way; walk in it.'"
Isaiah 30:21 NIV

April 7th, 2018

I'm confused on how my friend thinks that the devil is trying something when I so clearly feel that I need to choose God in all situations and that He is the way.

Dear Lord God,

Please continue to grant me peace in my days, give me my daily bread. Thank you for all you have given me, especially my three boys. Forgive me for not trusting you. I am here. Guide me. Love me. Grant me peace. I love you. I trust you. Amen.

"Give us each day our daily bread."
Luke 11:3 NIV

April 8th, 2018

I still can't understand, believe, acknowledge, want to know, that you're gone. Some days it's just not real. I still think you'll come back with us. It's all the nightmare I've been having and that I need to wake up even though I've done three months of stuff without you. Too many things without you. A vacation although you would have hated it. I'm feeling overwhelmed and full of loss. My heart is so broken right now with not knowing what to do if I'm doing okay. Am I right? Am I okay as a mom? I am trying to give it all to God, trusting he knows what's right.

Dear God,

I'm sorry for not seeking your help for myself. I'm so good at asking for others and really don't feel I deserve things. Thank you for giving me a brain that I can pray, read and write and do math and most of all teach and love it. Thank you for allowing me to make a difference, hopefully a tiny bit, with all the students I've had. Thank you for making me a mom and trusting me to guide me and love three of your own. Help me know what's right when to do what each of them how to love them yet guide them help me to show you to them, to pray for them, to give them more faith in you and your miracles and unconditional love. Help me grow in my trust for you. Help me see that all you do is good and has a purpose. Help me believe fully that Steve's death is for a reason, and that you know I've got this. Help me give you my burdens, my fears, my wants, my love, my trust. Help me be perfectly myself in the best version I can be. Thank you for the gift of my life, for Michael, Brian and Matthew, for my family and friends, for Hope, for Love & Faith, for your trust in me. Amen.

"And now these three remain: faith, hope and love. But the greatest of these is love."
1 Corinthians 13:13 NIV

April 9th, 2018

Thank you, God, for getting me out of bed today, for safety for everyone traveling this weekend, for honesty with family last night. Who knew I'd have to think about tombstones or headstones, plots, my kid's death and to have to think about remarriage? I guess I don't care about headstones, etc. I'd like to be buried by Steve. I don't think we need to decide about the boys right now. I think six plots is good. I really miss Steve, the laughter, his hugs, being able to put my cold toes on him, going for rides in the truck, eating together, everything. It's not real. Maybe I'm still in a nightmare and can't wake up.

I'm excited to see if I can have another experience. To know that God's plan is for me to always choose him over others, over the past and that is a choice. We still have free will, but it's also God telling me what he wants for me and for others too. I feel so connected to Steve and God when I'm in meditation. That feeling is good and holy.

"May my meditation be pleasing to him,
as I rejoice in the LORD."
Psalm 104:34 NIV

April 10th, 2018

Loss again. I can't imagine what their family is going through with the loss of their twelve-year-old son to an unknown cause. Losing Steve was awful, hard, scary and horrific, but he was forty-two. He had lived a life, had graduated, held a job, was married, had children, and had experiences like fishing, etc. At 12, you haven't experienced a lot yet and it really makes me wonder why God needs people more than us. What purpose is so important? Yet I know God has everything planned long before we even exist. I know that God sees all we do. It's part of what it's meant to be, but it's so confusing and frustrating.

God,

Thank you for the conversation at work, for time with family and friends and for your mother's intercession during the rosary, for your word, your miracles, your Son, and the Holy Spirit. Amen.

"God also testified to it by signs, wonders and various miracles, and by gifts of the Holy Spirit distributed according to his will."
Hebrews 2:4 NIV

During meditation, I felt God talking to me. 'Give me your burdens. Be still and listen. You are enough. Be the center of your world. Don't live for others. Be okay with yourself. The boys aren't going to be here forever, and you need to be comfortable with yourself."

A cup of miracles is an open name for a blog. I am excited and nervous to start to share my experiences. Steve walking with me. Steve being on the tractor. The rosary being in my pocket. The sunset when Julie J died. The Bruce story. Noah and the pig. The trinity in the precious blood. Seeing a bridge to choose moving forward with God. The right Bible verses for reflections. Matthew tasting blood with the Eucharist. Saying the rosary when grandpa passed away. Julie's story of the 's' block.

"Be still and know that I am God!"
Psalm 46:10 NLT

April 13th, 2018.

I wonder about Tuesdays. If subconsciously we can't do Tuesdays because it's the day when Steve died. It will be interesting to see next week if it happens again especially with it being 4 months.

I don't think we're burying Steve, it's just his body but it will be another good-bye. It will hopefully make this real. He is for sure gone and we're not getting him back. Maybe I need that for closure since I still struggle with knowing if he's gone. Wishful thinking. I know he's in heaven where God needed him to be; to look after my sister's baby, and the 12-year-old who died on Sunday. He needed to be there to get ready to welcome them.

I don't think our faith ever leaves us. We forget it but it's always there waiting for us to reconnect. God wants our love, trust, gratitude and honor. He is the only one who always stands beside us, alongside us, in front of us. We just need to ask. Being alone is not fun at all.

"I have come as a light to shine in this dark world, so that all who put their trust in me will no longer remain in the dark."
John 12;46 NLT

April 14th, 2018

Okay. Whatever. It is what it is. Be still. Deep breath.

"For the Spirit of God has made me,
and the breath of the Almighty gives me life."
Job 33:4 NLT

April 16th, 2018

The young boy that died is okay. He made it to heaven and is with Steve. I strongly felt Steve watching us yesterday at church. He was down on one knee telling a little boy, "That's my son Matthew and he's 11 like your brother. I get to watch over him just like now you get to watch over your brother." I need to call his mom and let her know.

There's a family that might be able to use Steve's clothes. They lost everything in a fire. What a loss that has to be.

The more reason I need to share miracles and works of the holy spirit that I experienced in the world.

"The Lord says, "I will guide you along the best pathway for your life. I will advise you and watch over you."
Psalm 32:8 NLT

April 17th, 2018

Today the reflection from Dynamic Catholic was really good. It was about removing self-worth from what is happening. God has a plan that's not based on how I feel about myself. I think I'm okay not being with the counselor maybe for a while, maybe other than to check on my goal but I think I'm near completion. I think with the other people that I'm working with plus my prayers and faith, my blogs and journaling, I have enough self-care right now and maybe that's what's meant to be. I need to do what I can and feel right now and not worry about what others or how it makes me feel about myself.

"Even if we feel guilty, God is greater than our feelings, and he knows everything."
1 John 3:20 NLT

April 20th, 2018

Happy anniversary! You finally asked me out 26 years ago today. I'm so glad I stopped at your house. I'm so glad I said yes that day, to your proposal, on our wedding day, to having kids, and to being in love. I miss you so much. I still can't believe you're gone. I can't believe you're not here every day or that you're not on a Lego trip or something. It's hard to be alone. I miss your touch, your teasing, your hugs, your love, our conversations and your advice. It's hard to be a single mom. It was hard when it was both of us making decisions but could figure it out together. I guess God knew that I could do this on my own. He knows I'm strong enough to make decisions, to love the boys, to guide them, to learn math, and hopefully to honor you. I love you. I can't imagine not loving you. Thank you for asking me out. You're the love of my life. Love me, now and forever.

"Love is patient and kind. Love is not jealous or boastful or proud." 1 Corinthians 13:4

April 22nd, 2018

I struggled to go to sleep last night. I napped a lot during the day and because Matthew was throwing up, he ended up sleeping on the couch, so I was alone. First night since Steve died. I think that's why. I sure miss our Sunday mornings together.

A friend sent me a sermon to watch on YouTube. I know God is working through us. I think the quiet part of healing is great. I love the counseling style too. I love the feeling of peace I have when I'm there. I need to let her know how I do more channeling to God and the Holy Spirit, to be like Christ, to go off and pray and that it is not the devil trying to reach me. I do feel Steve's presence when I am meditating. I wonder if my friends don't have miracles or experience so it's jealousy or unknowing that makes them curious or upset or worried about me. Maybe I'm supposed to lead these people that I know to meet with God. Maybe by being single, I can be more of a disciple than I've ever been before. I am a lecturer and plan to be a Eucharistic Minister. I do feel drawn to sharing my faith when I'm with these different people.

"I remember your genuine faith, for you share the faith that first filled your grandmother Lois and your mother, Eunice. And I know that same faith continues strong in you."
2 Timothy 1:5 NLT

I'm nervous about letting others get in my head. I'm excited to meditate to see if I can feel how I felt before when I've gone. I'm hoping I can get to the place on my own where I can be still and hear God and rest completely. I struggle with this at home.

"Take my yoke upon you.
Let me teach you,
because I am humble and gentle at heart,
and you will find rest for your souls."
Matthew 11:29 NLT

April 26th, 2018

I love hearing the owl or dove or whatever it is outside. I was hoping to see it but haven't. I pray the boys continue their relationship with God, go to church and witness miracles. I don't know why God took Steve home with him and away from us, but I trust the plan and know he's in heaven watching over all of us, all of the time, every day.

"There is more than enough room in my Father's home. If this were not so, would I have told you that I am going to prepare a place for you?" John 14:2 NLT

April 28th, 2018

Nervous, anxious, upset, overwhelmed, tired, and worried. Be not afraid. I'm trying to let it go and know what happens is meant to be. I know God's got this. Don't worry or be anxious over anything.

Dear God,

Give me the knowledge to pass the test today to get the math position for someone to take my current job if it is your will and it is according to my purpose. Please let me know that I'm okay either way. I know I can survive anything when I keep focus on you but it's hard sometimes like today. Please guide me as to how to support friends as she copes with others being pregnant even though they didn't want it or need it and she does. I know she'll be an awesome mom. Again, it's hard to trust you when life doesn't seem fair or right. How confusing to say I trust you but yet still question you? Is that right? Is it okay? Do you mind? I guess you already know. You know how many hairs I have on my head; you know that I'll pass today and that's why everybody says I've got this. I heard the owl today. A sign that it's all okay. Get out of this boat and walk towards me. I hear you. I love you. I'm so blessed to be connected to you. Help me collect enough for St Mary's Orphanage to be able to give the kids a future after they leave the orphanage. Give me the words to speak, the time to talk to your followers, and for others to connect where they are to. Guide me with an idea of how to present it and keep track of the amount collected. Thank you for bringing friends to church and helping her heal the wounds from when she was young. Thank you for keeping her sister's family safe during the fire. Amen

"And the very hairs on your head are all numbered. So, don't be afraid; you are more valuable to God than a whole flock of sparrows." Luke 12:7 NLT

I feel smart. Is that okay? I don't know how I feel about saying that. I don't usually compliment myself, but I do. Stacy said she'd never be able to do it. Amy said the same thing. I don't know why my brain gets it. God gives us something different and math is mine. I'm so glad the boys have that too.

"God has given each of you a gift from his great variety of spiritual gifts. Use them well to serve one another. Do you have the gift of speaking? Then speak as though God himself were speaking through you. Do you have the gift of helping others? Do it with all the strength and energy that God supplies. Then everything you do will bring glory to God through Jesus Christ. All glory and power to him forever and ever! Amen."
1 Peter 4:10-11 NLT

April 30th, 2018

I hear the owl. I think it's the same sound I heard this winter. Why at sunrise I wonder? Maybe it sings itself to sleep or something. Sometimes I wonder if it's all in my head or if I'm making it up or if it's the Holy Spirit communicating to me to get up and start the day and letting me know that everything was meant to be is going to be. A new song on the radio says, "if it's meant to be it'll be, baby, just let it be." A message from God. Be still and know that I am God. Be not afraid I go before you always. Come follow me and I will give you rest. Let your heart not be troubled. I've got this.

I really think Steve knew it was getting near the end by saying how old he felt. I think God needed him for the baby and for Jack. I think God takes us when we're done here, and he leaves others because we're either not ready for what he needs us for, or we're not done with our purpose here. Maybe drug dealers and murderers, because they don't know God, and can't go to heaven. Maybe it's our role to share God with them and once they find God and believe, they either turn their lives around or die and go to heaven.

I want Michael to go back to church. He's really struggling since Steve died and I hope it hasn't shaken his faith too much. Maybe with Mother's Day and the Bachelorette two weeks in a row will help and then not working other weekends too.

"Come to me, all you who are weary and burdened, and I will give you rest."
Matthew 11:28 NIV

May 1st, 2018

I think May 3rd is a day Steve first told me he loved me, and it wasn't until the next day that I told him. How quickly we went from friends to prom date to loving each other. I am so thankful God brought us together and even though we only had 26 years, it seems like a lifetime and now I'm in a new lifetime without him. There are still times that I can't, don't, want to believe he is gone. How come you won't come home? How come you can't wake up next to me in the morning? How come you're not here to talk to and get advice from? I'm lonely. I'm physically lost.

I need touch. Maybe that's why I'm seeking out chiropractic, massage and myofascial release. I just need the physical part in my life and although none of those are the same, it's still human contact and that's the hardest part of losing a spouse.

My sister asked me last night if I wanted to throw something at the TV and it took me a minute to figure out why. It has been a commercial where two kids fall in love and "I can't help falling in love" was the song playing. I get what she means, but I don't have the anger that others have a spouse. It makes me sad and jealous. Sad that that part of my life is missing and jealous that people can get a hug and I can't anymore.

"The wife does not have authority over her own body but yields it to her husband. In the same way, the husband does not have authority over his own body but yields it to his wife". 1 Corinthians 7:4 NIV

May 2nd, 2018

I needed to go to Matt yesterday for a hug. It didn't really work because it's not what I wanted or needed. So hard to miss someone and not be able to have that need met. Maybe that's why people remarry so quickly because of the touch piece. But I want it to be Steve, not just anyone. My head is pounding now.

Matthew was crying last night because he wants me at the dissection today, so much I'm going to see if someone can take my fifth hour off at work as unpaid or as a favor. I need to go and be with him. It hurts me to see all the boys hurt.

"No one should seek their own good,
but the good of others."
1 Corinthians 10:24 NIV

May 4th, 2018

I wonder if because Doug and Julie were here with Steve when he died if that's why it's hard for Matthew to be with them. Seeing Steve at the hospital and knowing that it was the last time we'd see him was really hard. I put my head on his shoulder and made tear stains on a shirt like I did in high school. Oh, what I wouldn't give to do it again.

"I have indeed built a magnificent temple for you, a place for you to dwell forever."
1 Kings 8:13 NIV

May 5th, 2018

Steve followed me part way home last night. I got out to my moms and went to the beach. On the way home, a truck like Steve's is suddenly behind me and then a couple of minutes later it was gone. I was listening to Bob Seger in the car. I don't know when it got there and then I didn't see it after I passed Wausau Road. It made me cry, but I felt comfort at the same time.

The sixth-grade girl wrote a really cool poem about Steve.

I found a grandpa rocking this within seconds of being on the beach which made me cry. So jealous that Steve and Grandpa get to see each other. I wrote a poem about being jealous of those in heaven watching over us together and yet we can't see them or hear them or touch them. The physical piece is hard. It makes sense to me why you would find someone else to be with or marry. There is such a loss, the loneliness, the emptiness, no one to vent to or get advice, no one to say they love you, no one to kiss or hug or cuddle with, no time alone on weekend mornings, no one to be at church and rub their knee. I want to go for rides at night and talk about everything and the romantic boat rides at sunset. I miss the teasing. No one to make coffee and breakfast sandwiches for. But I am strong. I have family and friends, co-workers and the boys. I have God. I have myself. I can journal. I can pray. I can make decisions. I can laugh and smile. I can go out with friends. I can be alone and be okay. I could do things for myself and by myself. I can love myself. I can be proud of myself.

"She is clothed with strength and dignity;
she can laugh at the days to come."
Proverbs 31:25 NIV

May 6th, 2018

I was dreaming and heard a noise at 3:54 am. I don't know if it was real or part of a dream. Now I can't sleep. I was searching Facebook and came across a post from 'Woman Living Well' called '10 verses for when you can't sleep'. The thing is, it's an old post from 2016 and it just appeared now. I know God is telling me to get some sleep and to quote a Matchbox 20 song, "you should get some sleep because tomorrow might be good for something".

I need to go to bed. I need to sleep. I need to pray and focus on hearing God. I need the rosary.

"And I am convinced that nothing can ever separate us from God's love. Neither death nor life, neither angels nor demons, neither our fears for today nor our worries about tomorrow— not even the powers of hell can separate us from God's love."
Romans 8:38 NLT

May 7th, 2018

Someone said that maybe gym class might be a physiological response that has Matthew's heart rate goes up and can trigger the memories of his heart racing at the hospital when Steve died. And he is not aware of the connection so that can be part of the problem with gym and maybe that's part of the basketball games too. The excitement mimics stress. Like Tuesdays subconsciously are hard for no other reason other than it's the day of the week. I remember Saturday's being hard when Tacy died too. For others I have no idea of the actual date or especially the day of the week that they passed away.

"Your survival rate for bad days is 100%." I think that quote sums up how I got through. I know I'll be okay. I know grief gets easier to cope with and the tears get less and less. I know it is God's plan for why everything happens or doesn't happen.

"A time to cry and a time to laugh.
A time to grieve and a time to dance."
Ecclesiastes 3:4 NLT

May 8, 2018

Almost 5 months. One book I was reading she said she knew the number of days, not just the weeks or that it was Tuesday.

I'm planning to see a Bob Seger tribute band on the 19th, how appropriate that is on the 19th and that it was all we listened to when we were first married.

"Teach us to number our days,
that we may gain a heart of wisdom."
Psalm 90:12 NIV

Why a fruit fly of all things to help us be aware to remember that Steve? A fruit fly? Only one in an odd place. Like right now in the bathroom. Or in the bedroom or the middle of the day or the middle of the night. In the kitchen makes the most sense, but why only one at a time?

Matthew seems to be healing. I think being with his friends helps to take his mind off of things and gets him out of the house too.

Steve got two awards this week. I wonder what will be said about me once I'm gone. Will I get all the awards like Steve is getting now or will they give a lot of them just because you died as more of a memory thing? I hope Steve is watching and knows that, no matter why they chose to give them now, you are an awesome teacher in all the schools you worked in and even at home with the boys and with me. You taught me so much about budgeting, parenting, marriage, relationships, and about myself. You are so loving, caring, kind, compassionate, and forgiving. I miss you very much and I so wish I could still go for truck rides and have conversations and more or go out to eat. I love how we could talk and did talk about everything and anything. I love you. I miss you.

"May the favor of the Lord our God rest on us;
establish the work of our hands for us—
yes, establish the work of our hands."
Psalm 90:17 NIV

May 10th, 2018

The chocolate chip video was yesterday's Facebook memory...it was so good to see you on video, but so hard to believe that you're really gone. Not sure when it will become real. Maybe the burial will help with that closure piece. Maybe I need to clean out your clothes and things like that.

"Jesus said to her, "Your brother will rise again." Martha answered, 'I know he will rise again in the resurrection at the last day.'"
John 11:23-24 NIV

Mom prom was really fun. I'm glad I went. I thought of Steve a couple of times and got hugged by a random person who turned out to be the mom of the girl who wrote the poem. She said her daughter still struggles to go to school some days. I think I'd like to go to his room again someday and see the kids, but I'm not sure when.

The casket and burial committing will be on Wednesday, the 16th at 10. I'm going. I'm taking another funeral day. I hope I can exchange the days off in January to be bereavement even though it wasn't funeral that I won't have an issue taking another day. I'm glad we got the contract changed for other people to 5 days for attending funerals, travel and the burial.

I give Jen a bracelet that says, 'be still and know' and a letter telling her that I don't know why she hasn't gotten pregnant but that God has a plan for her and then I pray she'll be a mom someday*, but that you'll always be a mom to some of the kids at school.

I tried to give Bec a Mother's Day card with a note telling her that I'd like to pay for her home study. I know she's a mom because she's had babies inside or even though they didn't survive to be with us. I don't understand it. I understand that less than Steve dying, I think. He lived a full life here on Earth, loving people, being loved and making a difference. Unborn babies are loved, and they never get to love others or have an earthly life. My faith tells me that God has a plan. I've never experienced that type of loss. I can't imagine being so excited and so much in love and then losing that life. I know the love part I immediately felt love for each of the three boys the moment I knew I was pregnant and then to lose the baby, I think hope, would be lost too. Losing Steve was unexpected, a shock unbelievable and hard but I guess you always know it's a possibility. I guess you know that you could lose a baby too. I don't know.

"Don't turn on the Jets in the hot tub till the water is above them. Just ask your mom". I overheard Stacy telling Matthew, referring to our honeymoon when Steve did that and shot water all over the hotel room. It was really funny. So many good memories of our time together. More happy than sad. Hard to be sad now sometimes too when I know he lived a happy life with us and now he has the ultimate happy life, he doesn't feel old and isn't in pain anymore. I'm sad for the memories he won't be part of. I'm sad that he won't be here in person to experience events with us. I know he's always watching over us and I'm sure laughing at us but yet understanding our pain from the loss. He lost enough people when he was here to understand what we're going through without him. Hard to believe it's been almost five months.

"He will wipe every tear from their eyes. There will be no more death or mourning or crying or pain, for the old order of things has passed away." Revelation 21:4 NIV

* Jen had a healthy baby boy in January of 2020

May 13th, 2018

My 18th Mother's Day

God,

Thank you for making me a mom to three amazing and wonderful boys. Thank you, Steve, for helping me raise them from conception. Thank you for saying yes to three. Thank you for taking care of Matthew when I couldn't go to the NICU. I feel for Julie today, her first Mother's Day without Steve. But she has Stacy and the boys. All three boys are going to mass with me today so I'm happy. Michael will go along next week for the baccalaureate. I hope it lets him see that he can do it even if it's hard. These two Sundays may also show him that it's easy and okay to be emotional. Amen.

Prayers for the passengers in the ambulance, the driver, EMTs and the medical team at the hospital. I wonder if they used the lights and siren for Steve? I would assume so. I wish we could have donated his organs. It would have been the ultimate way to save lives. He was an organ donor and always donated blood, but I guess he was without oxygen for too long or the organs would still be viable. Still really hard to believe that he's not at home while I'm here at the hotel.

"'Look! The virgin will conceive a child! She will give birth to a son, and they will call him Immanuel, which means 'God is with us.'"
Matthew 1:23 NLT

May 14th, 2018

I got a long necklace for Mother's Day and I'll still be able to wear Steve's ring on the gold chain at the same time. I think I'm getting ready to think about it being okay to not wear it every day. I also wonder about cleaning out the closet and dresser to be able to put some things away. Like the pile of books and some of the memory items, so the bedroom is free of clutter and could be more peaceful and relaxing.

What do I wear to the burial? I guess I'll need to see what the weather is like on Wednesday. I could just go in jeans I suppose. I think it's going to be good and yet really sad.

All the boys went to church yesterday, I'm sure to just make me happy. Beforehand, I got really upset, tears and then slammed the bathroom door and then gave it to God. I told Matthew, for him to tell his brothers that they didn't have to go to church if they didn't want to, that it was their decision. And although I still cried, I told God it was in his hands and that he would decide and give them the decision. I'm glad they were all there. It was comforting. I think I'm still hearing the owl. God's sign that we need to keep going.

"Those who worship the Lord on a special day do it to honor him. Those who eat any kind of food do so to honor the Lord, since they give thanks to God before eating. And those who refuse to eat certain foods also want to please the Lord and give thanks to God."
Romans 14:6 NLT

May 15th, 2018

Burials tomorrow. The principal was really confused about why there would be a burial now and it why it didn't already happen. He didn't understand that we don't do burials around in the winter because of the amount of snow we get. I wonder who else is being buried this week.

I know Steve is no longer here on Earth. I believe he is in heaven as a guardian angel watching over us, but it is still one more goodbye. It brings it all up again and makes it real again. I feel bad that Matt can't go. I feel bad that I haven't said anything to anyone else about it either. I think we'll invite anybody who wants to go for the service part with Father when that takes place. Do we wait for the stone to get back or just do it soon? I guess we will find out tomorrow.

> "Then an angel from heaven appeared
> And strengthened him."
> Luke 22:43 NLT

May 18th, 2018

I can't believe that Michael's done with high school. How does time fly by so quickly? Looking at a baby in the elementary pictures, it doesn't seem that long ago that he was born. I've done a lot in 18 years. Had a baby, switched jobs, had two more babies, bought a house, added on, got a master's degree, made new friends, lost family, celebrated, and grieved.

I never thought I would do the next 18 years alone. I know that I have family and the boys, but they are not Steve, a spouse, my best friend and soulmate.

Karen recommended for me to listen to "I'll be there" by the Escape Club. I remembered at the moment I read the artist's name. Listened before I went into church.

"The owl will nest there and lay eggs, she will hatch them, and care for her young under the shadow of her wings, there also the falcons will gather, each with its mate."
Isaiah 34:15 NIV

May 19th, 2018

5 months today. Maybe that's why this week's been hard.
Burial, awards, five months -no hugs, no advice, no emails.

The blessing of the grave will be on Thursday night at 6. Julie
will do snacky food at her house afterwards. I assume it's only
going to be a few minutes long at the cemetery, but
something the Catholic Church does, so I guess we'll go there
again. Part of me is not a cemetery girl. I know the person's
not there so why sit on a rock at a cemetery when I can talk to
them and pray with them anywhere? But I feel drawn to go to
pray the rosary there. Maybe I should go on the 19th of each
month and pray.

"Taking Jesus' body, the two of them wrapped
it, with the spices, in strips of linen. This was
in accordance with Jewish burial customs."
John 19:40 NIV

May 20th, 2018

I spent two hours at the cemetery yesterday morning, time alone in the truck listening to music, journaling, time by the grave praying the rosary and thinking. Took a couple of pictures and one had an orb, another single bird in the top of the tree.

"After the Sabbath, at dawn on the first day of the week, Mary Magdalene and the other Mary went to look at the tomb."
Matthew 28:1

May 22nd, 2018

The boys didn't go to school yesterday. Matthew missed 3 days last week too. It's been really hard. I feel okay when I'm there, but I'm also really tired. I spent most of the weekend feeling angry and crabby.

"Be angry, and yet, do not sin, do not let the sun go down on your anger"
Ephesians 4:26 NASB

May 23rd, 2018

I've been very crabby and negative since Friday especially at work. I've been less patient with the kids at school. I'm counting the days. I'm very worried about Brian.

I wonder about seeing someone this weekend or maybe going back to Jane. I know I need to pray more be quiet and listen to God, to be still, to journal, to ignore work, to not join in the negative talk, but it's hard when life has changed, when life sucks in a lot of ways. I need to do more with gratitude, affirmations, and get back to the compliment page in my journal too.

Scholarships this morning plus blessing of the grave tonight equals an emotional day. I'm stressed about speaking in front of everyone. I'm not looking forward to the blessing. It's just another formality. I think the burial was the closure. This is just another step.

I went to the beach today and spent two hours walking, relaxing, breathing and picking agates, Grandpa rocks and other weird stones.

I talked with Dad last night. He asked if I'm doing okay and told me to stay strong.

"Search for the LORD and for his strength. continually seek him." 1 Chronicles 16:11 NLT

May 25th, 2018

I presented the scholarships; my hands were shaking, and I cried. I went to the cemetery for the blessing.

Brian keeps telling me 'no shenanigans' if I start to cry. I hope he knows it's good to cry sometimes.

It's weird. Last night I had the windows open around the house because it was super-hot inside and as I was going to bed I almost asked Matthew, thinking he was Steve, if he'd hear the thunderstorm and close the windows. Ugh.

I wish you were here to close the windows and be upset about the yard and be worried about the house being presentable to everyone.

"But Martha was distracted by the big dinner she was preparing. She came to Jesus and said, "Lord, doesn't it seem unfair to you that my sister just sits here while I do all the work? Tell her to come and help me." But the Lord said to her, "My dear Martha, you are worried and upset over all these details!"
Luke 10:40 NLT

May 26th, 2018

Graduation day! Mixed emotions today. I'm sure all parents have it. Sad to see them grow up and move on with their life unknown and scary as to what will happen, questioning if we did enough, and wondering if we are going to be part of their lives still, and asking what the future holds. And yet so happy for them. They've completed school. They've done 13 or 14 years of classes and 18 years of growing up and now they choose the life they want to live.

I absolutely know he's watching over all of us and helping out with his strength, but it sucks to not have him here to celebrate big events.

Yesterday, I hugged Matthew and asked what he needed. He said he didn't know but nodded when I asked if he needed dad alive. He just cried... We both did.

I know that we did the best we could. I know God guided us. I know he'll always be around because of how we raised him. I hope I can raise Brian and Matthew enough on my own. I hope the 11 years Matthew saw us together is enough to show him how a marriage should be, and that education and faith are very important. I hope they learn a work ethic like we have. I hope their faith grows and they can live out their purpose.

"And Nehemiah continued, 'Go and celebrate with a feast of rich foods and sweet drinks and share gifts of food with people who have nothing prepared. This is a sacred day before our Lord. Don't be dejected and sad, for the joy of the Lord is your strength!'"

Nehemiah 8:10 NLT

I do wonder if Steve questioned going to heaven. Did he worry about leaving us? Did he wonder why now? Did he get to say that he wasn't ready or are you just so excited to be in heaven, see Jesus, see God, get to meet everyone that you lost again that being worried or being upset doesn't exist? Something I never thought about until yesterday. I know heaven is supposed to be beautiful and peaceful and without pain, but is it at that instant? Do you get to talk to Jesus about dying? Do you get to ask why or what about the ones I'm losing? Do you get there instantaneously when you die? I know people talk of purgatory, where the decision is made. For people like Steve who everyone knew was going to heaven, do they just get to go in. Is it like an elevator? We push the button and then Jesus is there to push the floor: hell purgatory, or heaven? Do you lose your clothes or is everyone in their most comfortable clothing? Do we see everyone in heaven as we knew them on Earth? Does everyone talk? Is time a factor there? All I know is that my goal is to live a life that allows me to be in heaven when God is ready for me to leave this world.

I told the boys that I was going to church yesterday. Michael said before bed that he was going to sleep in, so I didn't wake him up. I really missed them. I prayed about it and to think that I as a parent need to tell them they're going and that it's not a choice. They need their faith. Steve and I agreed on that and it needs to continue.

"'He will wipe every tear from their eyes. There will be no more death' or mourning or crying or pain, for the old order of things has passed away." Revelation 21:4 NIV

"The spirit is stronger, but the flesh is weak." is the topic of a video I watched on why it's hard to be disciplined. We need to pray before we make bad or healthy choices and allow our spirit to be stronger than our flesh. To follow Jesus, we must take up your cross daily and follow him by making sacrifices. We grow closer to God and his son and allow the spirit to do its job.

I wrote a thing and posted it on Facebook about not judging another parent even if you are one. You have no idea of the backstory or what they're going through. Offer prayers and support even if you disagree. I don't know if people will pick up the hint on this or not but it's out there and I truly feel that's how we should be anyway because we don't know what anyone is going through and what they have tried.

"Watch and pray so that you will not fall into temptation. The spirit is willing, but the flesh is weak." Matthew 26:41 NIV

May 30th, 2018

I feel lonely a lot of the time and empty feeling because something is missing. A huge part of my life. We were together so much longer than not together. I know he was my soulmate. I know we were meant to be together but I'm also angry that it was only 25 years. I'm upset that we don't get to celebrate our 25th or 50th wedding anniversary.

"Since they are no longer two but one, let no one split apart what God has joined together." Matthew 19:6 NLT

May 31st, 2018

I meditated yesterday. During it I heard a noise like a whistling wind blowing. Then I heard a car door and felt a spot of heat for a split-second on my wedding ring finger. I'm sure it was Steve watching over me.

"But watch out! Be careful never to forget what you yourself have seen. Do not let these memories escape from your mind as long as you live! And be sure to pass them on to your children and grandchildren."
Deuteronomy 4:9 NLT

I haven't heard the owl since the day we buried Steve. The fruit fly keeps appearing and then disappearing. Again, the shower curtain clung to me while I showered. It doesn't happen the whole shower nor does it matter if I have the fan on or not. I know they are all signs that Steve is okay and watching us.

"The Lord says, "I will guide you along the best pathway for your life. I will advise you and watch over you." Psalm 32:8 NLT

June 5th, 2018

Positive. Be positive. See the good. Connect to God. I got this.
Four more days till school is out.

"Taste and see that the LORD is good;
blessed is the one who takes refuge in him."
Psalm 34:8 NIV

June 8th, 2018

Last day of my 20th school year. Had a good time at the Calumet party last night. Some tears but lots of laughter which I needed. We were talking about babies and Julie said that she got quiet because she told Steve to just go for it as far as me wanting another baby, to try for a girl but he always said we were too old. I can't imagine raising a baby right now on my own. I'm so grateful the boys are as old as they are so they can have memories of Steve but also had enough time to learn from him to know his expectations and desires for them.

"It will be like a woman suffering the pains of labor. When her child is born, her anguish gives way to joy because she has brought a new baby into the world."
John 16:21 NLT

June 9th, 2018

I've been awake for a while praying that God stops my brain for me and thinking of work, but I can't. I'm upset. I'm scared. I'm angry. I'm worried. There have been too many things over this year that are wrong or disturbing.

I'm not wanting to use my grief as an excuse, but I know it's affecting me. It obviously has changed my energy levels, etc. but I also took time off while still working, attending conferences, emailing, etc. because I'm dedicated. Maybe I should have taken a semester off, but I know the students need me and I needed them. Was I the best teacher this past 5 months? No. Am I upset by that? Yes.

I want to be the best teacher and mom I can be, but I also lost my best friend and the love of my life, the partner I raised my boys with, my rock. How can I not change? I can hardly get out of bed most days, but I know I had support from the teachers, the kids and the parents and it allowed me to go on many days. I felt when I walked out yesterday thinking that other than cleaning up my room I was leaving for the last time, that I won't get the math job and I will have to leave.

"Worry weighs a person down;
an encouraging word cheers a person up."
Proverbs 12:25 NLT

Dear God, thank you for making me a teacher I am. Thank you for 20 years of making a difference. Please guide me and let me know the plan you want me on. Are the boys going to be okay? Can I move out Steve's clothes? Am I ready? I can't take the body wash out of the shower yet, maybe never. I need that smell. I need to remember him. I can eat foods he liked or made. I can hear his voice on the answering machine. I can see pictures and videos. I can smell body wash and deodorant. But I can't feel him. I sense his present. Brian teases me and makes comments like Steve. We do events and things like we used to, but I can't feel him. Through all this I just want a hug from him and to have him say, it's okay, that I'm doing the right thing, that I am strong. I know that I only need support and love from you, God and that you do love and support me. I need to help letting go and allowing you to guide me. Here I am Lord. Is it I Lord? Continue to bless me. Continue my life. Lead me Lord. Lead me on the right path while I dwell on Earth and to get to heaven. You are the prince of peace. Bless me with your peace. You tell me not to worry just so I'll turn to you? I know I need you. I know you are my strength, that I can do all things because you strengthen me. I love you. You are my rock and my salvation. With you I am enough. I am strong. I am faith filled. I am a believer. I experience miracles. I love you Lord. I need you. I put myself in your hands. Amen

"Then I heard the voice of the Lord saying, 'Whom shall I send? And who will go for us?' And I said, 'Here am I. Send me!'"
Isaiah 6:8 NIV

June 21, 2018

I missed the 6-month anniversary of Steve's death. I don't know how since usually dates stick in my head. I think that's the day I went to the bank, so I know I wrote the date, but it never clicked maybe it means I'm healing. Saturday is Steve's birthday, and no one is sure what to do. I think maybe I'll call Matt and see if we can burn boxes and drink tequila. Mass is for him on Sunday because Saturday was already taken.

"But the crowds learned about it and followed him. He welcomed them and spoke to them about the kingdom of God and healed those who needed healing."
Luke 9:11 NIV

June 23, 2018
Happy 43rd birthday Steve!

Do you celebrate birthdays in heaven or is December 19th, the day that you got there now your birthday? Your alarm went off this morning, I wonder if it was just you saying hello. I really miss you. Your sense of humor, your smile, your teasing, but also your touch and hugs. I also miss your advice but maybe I am meant to make more decisions on my own. Your mom is planning a picnic for you today which I think is weird because you didn't like them, but it must make sense to her. I'm not sure I want to go, but if she's happy, I guess why not. I thought about making carrot cake today and inviting people over, also something you wouldn't want. I love you. I miss you and I'm jealous of you being with God.

"Pharaoh's birthday came three days later, and he prepared a banquet for all his officials and staff. He summoned his chief cup-bearer and chief baker to join the other officials."
Genesis 40:20 NLT

June 28, 2018

Happy 21st anniversary. I still love you. The length of your "Love of a lifetime" will be only 20 years; 26 if you count when we started dating. I hope and pray all three boys find their soulmate and a love of their lifetime. I wish you were here to help me decide what to do.

What I miss most is your hugs when I'd tuck myself in and you'd hold me till I felt better then you'd make some sort of comment to make me laugh or start to tip over. I need that safety now and I know that I need to turn to God, that all along I should have turned to God. He's always been there.

I wonder if you're with Kenny today. It would be 43 years for him and Karen. I picture you talking about how much you miss us and love us and wish you could be here.

I wish we could be with them and as much as it's my goal, my dream, my purpose, I'm not ready. I need to be with the boys, support others, still affect school kids, etc. I'm not sure God is done with me. I don't know or understand his wants and plans, but I do believe that he has it all worked out for each one of us, every one of us, on when to take us home to be with him and to be reunited with everyone we've lost.

"So, whether we are here in this body or away from this body, our goal is to please him."
2 Corinthians 5:9 NLT

June 29, 2018

Dear God,

Please guide me to do what is right for me and for the boys.
Help me see the plan you have laid out before me. Take my
worry and anxiety again. Continue to bless me. Continue to
allow me to come to you blessed and broken. Thank you for
the gifts you've given me. You are amazing and wonderful. I
need to praise you more. Help me feel comfortable doing that.
Help me show you to the world. Amen.

"They will not get tired or stumble. They will
not stop for rest or sleep. Not a belt will be
loose, not a sandal strap broken."
Isaiah 5:27 NLT

July 6, 2018

Matthew has been very quiet lately, but I feel like I have been too. I still feel very alone and lonely even when I'm with people. 25 years of having him with me at most events, most of the time and we were never apart for more than four or five days.

Maybe Steve was just too tired to go on anymore. He never slept right after the drunk driver came through our house. He was always able to hear every little noise in the house or outside. He couldn't get comfortable, especially at the end with his belly button and his shoulder. He just kept saying he was getting old at 42. I think God was preparing all of us, but we didn't pay attention or listen or notice like we should have. I hope he's watching over us and shaking his head. I hope he sees us moving forward, but still grieving. I hope he sees the impact he made on all of us, me, the boys, his family, the school, the church, and the community.

"Do you not know? Have you not heard? The LORD is the everlasting God, the Creator of the ends of the earth. He will not grow tired or weary, and his understanding no one can fathom." Isaiah 40:28 NIV

July 9, 2018

Who knows what this year will bring for me and the boys too?
No one has talked about moving out of the house and I'm
good with staying. I can see myself at some point selling and
getting something smaller, but not now. I love the house. We
made it what we wanted and designed it to be here forever. I
still get upset when I think that we won't celebrate our 25th or
50th anniversaries. I think what we had was good and strong. I
hope that I can be an example to the boys. I hope we were
loving to each other in front of others that they want that too.
Without
God, our marriage wouldn't have worked. It's how we got
through arguments, pregnancy, money issues and raising the
boys. All because we have faith in God and his plan for us as
much as sometimes it didn't make sense.

"He replied, "If you have faith as small as a
mustard seed, you can say to this mulberry
tree, 'Be uprooted and planted in the sea,' and
it will obey you." Luke 17:6 NIV

I had an amazing experience yesterday. I prayed. I asked God to let my brain quiet enough to be able to hear Jesus. I pretended that he was there as a friend. So many things I've read say to do that. Well it worked. I felt that Jesus was with me. The white light I often see was on my left side and suddenly light was coming from that side too. I was thinking about things and Jesus gave me answers. He said that he needed Steve to be in heaven with him to watch over the babies. And that also he had prepared Steve by having him stop committees and less commitments so that he could be home with us more. He told me to go back and look at my journals from September to December and see what we had more us time and then we went on more dates. He then told me that it was okay that I live alone and that I could be happy. He advised me to go to Arizona with Michael, to get a hotel night with a pool for Matthew and do something alone with Brian too. To not worry what others, think and to do what I feel is right and to be a mom first and foremost. It was really peaceful and quiet. I have no idea if it lasted 2 minutes or 20 minutes. I was just laying on my bed. The other thing that he told me was that the hand I felt on my side was his hand. You said he chose that place to hold me because I had asked for healing that day. My side was the place he chose because it was his side being pierced when he was on the cross.

"Instead, one of the soldiers pierced Jesus' side with a spear, bringing a sudden flow of blood and water." John 19:34 NIV

July 16, 2018

Prayerfully hoping that God's plan is revealed to me soon. I just read that worrying is worshipping a problem and if we're worshipping the problem, we can't worship God at the same time. It makes sense. I pray that I can continue to give my worries to God.

Please Lord Jesus take away my anxieties, give me peace, let your plan be made known. Help me feel at peace and be still in your grace and love. Allow your purpose for my life to be fulfilled. Help me feel confident in my skills and abilities. Help me heal from my illness by taking time with your word and the words of others that guide me to be the best version of myself. Forgive me for worrying and being angry and upset when I know I should let go and be faithful to you and your will on your time schedule.

"In him we were also chosen, having been predestined according to the plan of him who works out everything in conformity with the purpose of his will." Ephesians 1:11 NIV

July 30, 2018

Interview today. I'm really trying to just give it all to God. To have faith that it is what it is. His plan for me is already set and I need to let go of my control and give it to God. I need to accept what happens and go with what happens. I'm trying to be confident and to let go of self-doubt but there's this question of what if I don't get it, then what? Whatever God's plan is, is what I'll do.

Thank you, God, for being in control so I don't have to be. Thank you for having my best life as your plan. Help me show how much I love you by being strong and honest today and every day. Amen.

"For this very reason, make every effort to add to your faith goodness; and to goodness, knowledge; and to knowledge, self-control; and to self-control, perseverance; and to perseverance, godliness; and to godliness, mutual affection; and to mutual affection, love." 2 Peter 1: 5-7

July 31, 2018

Spent time crying last night and looking at pictures and reading love letters. So hard. I can't hear your voice or picture you anymore. I need to record your voice from the answering machine. I'd love to hear your advice on a lot of things. I miss you. I've been doing okay most of this month. But last night was hard again. Maybe because I'm seeing a friend today and we're going to ride to the cemetery, and I haven't been there since the stones have been placed. I feel like I'm starting to help others grieve. It's weird to go places without you. I'm so lost without you sometimes and other times I feel in control and stronger because I have to make the decisions and be the one in charge. I don't always feel like I'm doing a good job. I've been really tired lately and hope it's because of all the travel in time in the car. You'd be proud of me for driving from Arizona and then across the Mackinac Bridge. It felt good to do those things and to show the boys that you can overcome your fears. I wish the boys got to know you longer. I wish they got to hear you say you were proud of them one more time. I wish they had letters from you like I do. I will love you forever.

"If a man has a hundred sheep and one of them wanders away, what will he do? Won't he leave the ninety-nine others on the hills and go out to search for the one that is lost?"
Matthew 18:12 NLT

August 10, 2018

I think I'm going to be able to add pieces of my faith to my office, which is exciting. I always felt I couldn't in my classroom.

I'm also going to be able to parent full-time when I need to be. That was supposed to be our job together.

Had to mark single on my new tax forms and insurance paperwork and it sucks.

Drove the truck down the canal last night thinking of when we were in high school stopping to make out. I really miss the physical contact. I think that's why the healing, chiropractic, massage, myofascial release, etc. are so important.

"It is God who arms me with strength
and keeps my ways secure."
2 Samuel 22:33 NIV

August 12, 2018

Hope. I think I need to Hope more. I have been telling myself to not worry, to let go and let God. It is what it is. But I wonder if I'm forgetting hope. My daily reflections the past two days have been about hope and I think I need that. I hope the boys return to church. I hope this week goes well. I hope I can do my new job well. I hope people having surgery are well and heal. I hope to get to heaven. I hope to see Steve again. I hope I can start to make a meal plan and stick with it. I hope I can heal physically. I hope I can continue on my faith journey and share with others.

Hope. Peace. Love. Faith. Trust. I trust God's plan. I hope for peace and love. I have faith.

"Three things will last forever—
faith, hope, and love—
and the greatest of these is love."
1 Corinthians 13:13 NLT

August 13th, 2018

I think I'm getting depressed now. I really want to just lay in bed watching TV and surfing social media. I don't really want to journal or pray. I feel alone. I miss Steve. Church is hard without him or the boys. I felt lonely yesterday. Then the song for the offertory was First Corinthians made into a song. Then they're all these families trying to control their kids and it's the moms that seem to do that more of the correcting. It was so different with our boys. Steve did all the discipline. He was always the bad guy and I was too coddling. I think I'm doing it again. I need to be creative instead of vegging in my bed. It's not helping my neck, my back or hips either.

"'Each of you must show great respect for your mother and father, and you must always observe my Sabbath days of rest. I am the LORD your God.'" Leviticus 19:3 NLT

August 20th, 2018

I just know God has a plan. The more I listen to Him in church or notice what I hear, the better I feel. I don't think the boys have that connection and that's what I want. I want them to experience miracles, to see how God answers prayers every day, for the peace he gives. I want them to have God when they have no one else. Maybe a different building or a different priest would help and maybe Saturday or Sunday night would also help. Maybe being back in school with the routine would help. I worry about their health, their money, and their faith. I worry even though God tells me not to.

God take over!

"Therefore, do not worry about tomorrow,
for tomorrow will worry about itself.
Each day has enough trouble of its own."
Matthew 6:34 NIV

August 22nd, 2018

I'd like to go on a walk on the beach right now by myself, but I
don't know if it's okay to do that. Will others be hurt or
worried or will they not care? Why do I worry about what
others think? Why do I want them to worry about me? Is it
normal to want someone to care about you and your feelings?
Maybe that's what I need to talk to a counselor about.

"They do not fear bad news; they confidently
trust the LORD to care for them."
Psalm 112:7 NLT

August 26th, 2018

I talked with Cathleen yesterday and she told me that she can tell based on how I talk that I am strong and doing well with my grief and that I am a good mom. She also told me that I should tell people how much talking with someone has helped me and maybe it would convince others to go and see someone. I do feel strong, I guess, but I also don't think I have a choice. Steve would want me to go on. The boys need me. I need to live. I have no control of anything. It's God's plan and I need to follow him and do what he says I need to do. I can only do so much as a mom. I can encourage and love my boys but it's really up to God. I know he gave them to me for me to love and to raise. I wouldn't trade them for anything. I wouldn't change my life with Steve either. I'm so glad he just went quickly when God needed him.

I regret not saying goodbye in the morning or giving him one last kiss that day. I regret teasing him about his life insurance policy. One of the things I really loved about him was a sense of humor. I miss being teased. I miss him being silly with the boys. I miss raising our boys together. I miss his advice and loving heart. I miss him bringing an elephant ear from the fair. I miss and making us go to church together as a family. I really miss him making the boys help out around the house. I know I've got this. I know I can do it. The sun pouring in right now confirms that. God's got this. Let go. Be still. Have Peace. Love never ends.

"The faithful love of the LORD never ends!
His mercies never cease."
Lamentations 3:22 NLT

August 27th, 2018

A friend of mine was at the fair yesterday and told me how great it is that I'm doing so well. I feel like I am for the most part. After she left my mom gave me a hug while crying, saying that she knows how hard it is even though I looked fine. I really was fine.

I think the new job is really helping. It gives me a new focus or something to be excited about instead of grieving. I think the binge-watching of TV is my grief right now. It lets me live in an alternate world. In one episode a doctor is able to touch and talk to her dead fiancé. I don't think people return as a physical body that's invisible to others, but I do feel Steve's presence here. I often sense a shadowy movement out of my peripheral vision, especially in the front porch if the door is open. I also see it in the office by the fish tank when I'm in my bed. Yesterday and other days, the sunlight changed while I was writing. The shower curtain moves against me in the shower. I'd love to feel him. I wonder if he's one of the angels that did touch me.

Yesterday, during the Our Father, I had my head bowed and was whispering the prayer with tears and all of a sudden my white light on my left got brighter and I felt my head being lifted to have my face up towards the light and felt comfort and peace.

"He responded, 'The LORD, in whose presence I have lived, will send his angel with you and will make your mission successful. Yes, you must find a wife for my son from among my relatives, from my father's family." Genesis 24:40 NLT

August 28th, 2018

I wish other people would see someone. I need them to be okay with me being okay. I know I can be okay without them understanding, but it would make me feel better if others were in a better spot to like me and I think the boys are. God has got this. God says be still and know that I am God.

"No one should seek their own good, but the good of others." 1 Corinthians 10:24 NIV

September 10th, 2018

Had a hard time at church yesterday but then experienced peace when "Perfect" was on the radio. I visited with friends and helped out and heard "Right Here Waiting" on the radio. Little signs that Steve is okay.

I know God needed him. I know he was hurting here and feeling old. I'm not sure why or if I'll ever know, but I do know I'm thankful for the time we were together in the life we created and for our boys. I hope they're okay for real and it's not just a cover up for me or someone else. They seem okay. They seem happy. They seem adjusted.

I think Steve gave the boys what they needed: skills, love, vision, and knowledge of life in faith and how to be a dad. I think the connection with the grandpas too and now having an uncle also will help. I think they're going to be fine. I think they'll get married and be loving supportive husbands and great dads because they'll know that time is precious, and they'll make memories with their families in case they too are taken sooner than anyone thought would happen. I don't know if the surgery had anything to do with his death, but it doesn't matter. Life is not in our control. God made us to be here for a certain length of time to fulfill his purpose for us and when we're done that, he takes us back with him. Thank you, God, for giving us Steve and for taking him home with you. Amen.

"Therefore, keep watch, because you do not know the day or the hour."
Matthew 25:13 NIV

September 19th, 2018

9 months today. I'm not sure what I feel. Sad to not be making new memories, grateful for the memories I have the time we did have, jealous of you being in heaven not in pain not feeling old, not tired, or confused on why God needed you now and lonely. Being a single mom is hard and I guess I question if I'm making the right decisions or if I'm too easy and let too much go because they're grieving. I don't think I'm angry. I don't think I'm scared anymore. I was scared to be alone, scared to make decisions, scared of how to feel. But I feel better now that I realize God doesn't ever give us more than we can handle and so I tell myself that God took you home with them because he needed you to watch over the kids he knew were coming. He knew I could do this on my own and that I'd be okay and that through this I would get stronger, more confident, be able to help others, make okay decisions, learn new things and be okay. That I can be happy. I can laugh. I can smile and say I'm fine and mean it. But I can forget you're gone sometimes and that's okay. That the boys will be okay. God has a plan for them too and although I still don't think it's fair that they don't get to make new memories. They got enough love and teaching from you, that they'll be okay. They'll be fine. They'll be good. God knows best and we're all here to fulfill his purpose for our lives until he takes us home too.

"But the Lord answered her, "Martha, Martha, you are worried and troubled about many things, but one thing is needed. Mary has chosen the best part; it will not be taken away from her." Luke 10: 41-42 NLT

September 24th, 2018

Miracles yesterday. When I was finishing showering, the shower curtain moved to touch my leg and I immediately started singing, " I know you are here standing always at my side" that usually starts with Yahweh but I felt it was Steve. Then during the "Our Father", my left hand was raised, and I felt like it was being held. My fingers were pressed together and across my hand it was colder. I think Steve was there holding my hand. God's plans are perfect.

"Yet you are near, LORD,
and all your commands are true."
Psalm 119:151 NIV

September 29th, 2018

I think my friends need to see a marriage counselor. It makes me so mad because I'd do anything to be able to go out to dinner with Steve or talk to him about my day. I miss our relationship so much. I miss driving around and laughing. I miss crying and being held in his arms. I miss hearing stories. I miss going to dinner. I miss romantic nights at a hotel and the Saturdays hanging out and Sunday mornings. I miss making him coffee. I miss raising the boys together. I miss him. I love him. I miss our marriage. I miss our love. I miss his touch, his smile, his hugs, getting flowers on a bad day, giving foot rubs watching baseball, being teased and picked on, even him being stressed and crabby.

"When the dead rise, they will neither marry nor be given in marriage; they will be like the angels in heaven." Mark 12:25 NIV

September 30th, 2018

Everything comes from God. Everything is in his control. What I sense and feel is because of him. What he knows, I need to experience. He knows I need to talk with somebody and that I need to be healed through prayer and meditation. I do think crystals, stones and healing rods aren't needed to connect with God but if that's what it takes for somebody else to feel that they need to pray, then it's working. Catholics use rosary beads to pray. We use candles for everything, even when we have electricity. We use certain chalices and plates and why does the container make a difference? Can't we just use our fingers to pray the rosary? The wine would still turn into Jesus's blood if it was in a plastic cup, right? And all of this could happen if it was dark on a beach somewhere. It's all about faith and belief and what the symbols and objects represent not the actual items. God is my choice, my first and my only choice. God is in control of my life, my thoughts, and my actions. God put me here for a purpose and right now I believe it's to share him and his miracles with the world. One Instagram post or blog or by teaching but to share how he has worked in my life to bring me the peace I feel and to bring me more joy than anything else.

"And he took a cup of wine and gave thanks to God for it. He gave it to them and said, "Each of you drink from it, for this is my blood, which confirms the covenant between God and his people. It is poured out as a sacrifice to forgive the sins of many."
Matthew 26:26-27 NLT

October 3rd, 2018

Mary, thank you for being with me yesterday and always. And for your wisdom, guidance, and experience showing me that it will work out if I trust in God, and say yes to what he's asking of me. Knowing I don't have the answers, but that he does. That I can't and I'm not supposed to do this on my own. But I have your experience to guide me. You said yes to carrying Jesus, to giving birth, to feeling your country, to letting him go to preach and create disciples. You encouraged his first miracle. You were there when he was crucified and died. Oh, the grief you must have felt and also the love you had and the trust that it was all for God's purpose and part of his plan. I need your strength and love of God and of Christ and your trust that the Holy Spirit will guide me as to what I'm supposed to go and do. I've got this. I can be a good mom to these three boys. I can be a grandma. Grandma Rachel made it 30 years as a widowed Mom and Grandma. I can do it too. I need to let go, to let God and to allow the boys to make decisions and trust that they'll be okay. We taught them and raised them to have faith. We took them to church every weekend and for holy days. They were altar servers. They've heard my stories and they see examples before and then trust and faith in my grief. They know they can come to me and no matter what choices they've made.

"Mary responded, "I am the Lord's servant. May everything you have said about me come true." And then the angel left her."
Luke 1:38 NLT

November 4th, 2018

Today is the All Souls Day Mass at church. Families walk up to
the altar carrying a candle and then Father puts a candle on
the altar and gives a wooden cross with your loved one's
name on it. I don't know if I want to go up at all. I don't know
if I want to go alone. I don't know if I want support. I don't
know. I also don't feel like crying and that surprises me. I feel
like it's just one more thing to go through.

Dear Lord Jesus,

You wept when your friend Lazarus died. Did you accept
support from those around you? Did you just go off by
yourself and want to be that way? Help me know what's right
to do. Help me not hurt myself or others. Help me have the
strength to walk down the aisle one more time without him
but to meet him at the altar like when we got married and I
walked with my parents so now I walk with his parents. Thank
you for the guidance now and always. Amen

"When Jesus saw her weeping, and the Jews
who had come along with her also weeping, he
was deeply moved in spirit and troubled.
"Where have you laid him?" he asked. "Come
and see, Lord," they replied. Jesus wept."
John 11:33-35 NIV

November 5th, 2018

I punched the shower wall yesterday. Mad that Steve is gone. Not at God. Not at Steve. Just the situation. I cried and cried. I put body wash on the wall to smell and just leaned against it and cried.

"The Lord is compassionate and gracious, slow to anger abounding in love."
Psalm 103:8

November 17th, 2018

God put us all here for a purpose. We are all here to live out that purpose and be here as long as we are needed to be. God knows all of it already. He knows how we're going to live and what we're going to do. He gave us free will to make choices but knows the effects of them before we make the choice. He always wants us to choose good, light, him, Jesus and to pray. To be still and let him be in control. He loves us so much. I can't wait to be with him in heaven.

"The Lord himself goes before you and will be with you; he will never leave you nor forsake you. Do not be afraid; do not be discouraged."
Deuteronomy 31:8 NIV

November 21st, 2018

Be still and know that I am God. She gave me homework to breathe and do legs up the wall. During my yoga session last night, I was laying on my back and my hand was on my jacket. I felt like Steve was there holding my hand. I also felt his presence behind me. I think he's saying I've got this, and he didn't leave me alone. God also told me that He wouldn't have made me be a single mom if he didn't think I could handle it and that he knows I'm strong enough. Steve and I did enough together that I can do this now on my own.

"In peace I will lie down and sleep, for you alone, LORD, make me dwell in safety."
Psalm 4:8 NIV

Help me Lord live according to your will. Help me grieve and experience Joy. Help me know how to support and love my boys. Continue to bless me with miracles. I love you. I can't wait to live with you in the place you created for us. Amen. I do.

"Do not be like them, for your Father knows what you need before you ask him. "This, then, is how you should pray: "'Our Father in heaven, hallowed be your name, your kingdom come, your will be done, on earth as it is in heaven."
Matthew 6: 8-10 NIV

December 8th, 2018

I think I heard God last night. I heard him as I was listening to the rosary trying to fall asleep which normally works, but not last night. It was the sorrowful mysteries and I thought about Jesus being beaten with the reed. He told me how much he suffered and sacrificed for me. He did it so I wouldn't have to suffer. I feel that I am suffering, that I worry a lot, that I don't pray enough, that we're not praying the right way or for the right things, but I also feel like I have finally accepted that Steve is not coming back.

I'm on my own and I can do this. This is my purpose. To continue to raise three boys on my own. To continue not just raise. Steve and I started this together. At the start you did a lot of the discipline, and getting them to church and to do chores, because he wanted them to grow up to be amazing husbands or dads. I hope they had that example long enough and that through his love and teaching and now with the Grandpa's that they continue to grow into amazing men and follow God's plan for them.

Dear Lord Jesus,

Work with the hearts and minds of all three boys and bring them to you. Help to open their eyes to see the good that you do and the love that you give no matter what the circumstances are. Help heal others so they return to you too. Help me be an example to them. Help me know how to share you, your mother Mary and the saints with them daily. Help me be your servant to live according to your will. Thank you for the millions of blessings you've given me. Thank you for Steve, his family, the boys, marriage and the promise of eternal life with you in heaven. You are amazing and awesome. You saved us all. You created us. You came to Earth and witnessed the sorrows and healed the sick. Help me be like you to be able to go off and pray. Thank you for this weekend to let me hear your voice and feel your presence. Guide me to live as you intend. Continue to bless me with miracles and give me a way to share them with not only my voice but with the world. Thank you for the sunshine to let us know it won't always be dark and cloudy. Thank you for making Steve's presence known to me. Show him and his constant love and protection to the boys too. I love you. I love your promise. I love your father. I love that your mother said yes to God. Help me be like her always. Amen

"Very early in the morning, while it was still dark, Jesus got up, left the house and went off to a solitary place, where he prayed."
Mark 1:35 NIV

December 9th, 2019

Steve, I hope you didn't feel neglected that I spent time with the boys over you sometimes, more often than maybe I should have. Our marriage kind of got put on hold when we became parents on top of spouses. I loved being married to you, parenting with you, even though it was really hard, and we had our disagreements. You were right. You knew how to raise the boys to be gentlemen, to be kind, to be smart and helpful. Thank you for pushing me. Thank you for showing me your faith and how important it is. I know you're watching over all of us and I hope you can do that even when we're miles apart this weekend. Help the boys see that you were right to make them go, to help me make them go to church, even though they were bigger than me. Help us celebrate you. Help us get through Christmas. Help me know if I should put out my stocking or not. Continue to love us forever for now.

"But you, LORD, do not be far from me. You are my strength; come quickly to help me."
Psalm 22:19 NIV

I had an awesome experience yesterday. I was able to witness Jesus in the garden, being scourged, carrying the cross, falling, being on the cross and then resurrected. Birds were singing. It was a blue sky with even a cool breeze now and then. Jesus told me "come follow me" and "take my yoke and I'll take yours".

"Take my yoke upon you and learn from me, for I am gentle and humble in heart, and you will find rest for your souls. For my yoke is easy and my burden is light."
Matthew 11:29-30 NIV

December 19th, 2018

One year.

365 days of grief.

Hard to believe we've made it that long without you. I still expect you to be driving your truck home from school. I feel weird today, sad but also some relief. Like it's going to be okay because we've come this far and are doing okay, even well. I feel sad knowing it's going to be a lot more years till I see you. Part of me wants to come today to be with you and God but the other part of me needs to stay here to be with the boys, family, and friends.

I chose joy as my 2019 word because I feel that that's missing a lot in the past year. I did feel peace a lot over this year and everyone says I'm strong so my 2017 and 2018 words must have been appropriate too.

I want to love and support today, but I want it every day, not because it's been a year since you got to go home. I know you're happier there than you ever could have been here, but I hope part of you misses us. I hope you hesitated a teeny bit when God came for you. I hope you told you that would be okay. Thank you for being an amazing friend first, then a husband and finally a dad. You taught us all so much and continue to do so. I know you wouldn't want us to sit around and mourn for you. But you also have known me well for 25 years and know that dates are in my brain and that today would be hard.

I think I've surprised you. I think we planned that we'd have enough money for me to take time off and that I'd go back to work eventually. I think I've done better than either of us thought. I do worry about money but shouldn't have to because you set it all up so that we can live the same lifestyle we had. I know right now you're shaking your head at me for lying in bed in tears and the amount I spent on Christmas gifts this year and at the boys for not helping around the house as you taught them, but I also feel your love. I know you are here with us even though we don't see you or hear your voice except on recordings. I know you're watching over us always waiting for our purpose to be fulfilled.

I worry about others and if I'm there enough for them. I want to be supportive of others' grief but it's like I'm a measuring cup and I only have so much to give to grief and I give a huge majority to myself and then to the boys. There is not much left to give anyone else after that, but it bothers me sometimes. I know this is really hard for so many people I know they're hurting too, and I don't know how to help them. I don't know if I should stop by and see those locally. If I should text or call those away from here because I know everyone also wants to know how I'm doing and to take care of me too. My heart breaks thinking of your family, your friends, your colleagues and members of the church and community. Keep watching us. I can hear you tell us to 'suck it up buttercup' and also that 'you're good'. I'm so happy you're not in pain anymore and that you don't feel old like you did when you were here. I'm so happy you experienced the ultimate joy every day. I love you. I miss you.

"Here are some of the parts God has appointed for the church: first are apostles, second are prophets, third are teachers, then

those who do miracles, those who have the
gift of healing, those who can help others,
those who have the gift of leadership,
those who speak in unknown languages."
1 Corinthians 12:28 NLT

December 22nd, 2018

Yesterday the shower curtain moved really weird. I wasn't in it. And then I had my playlist on shuffle. "Love of a Lifetime" came on then "You'll Accompany Me" and then "Perfect". I know God was sending me the message that I'll be with Steve again.

"We know that we will be together because our love is strong." "You'll walk with me, talk with me, where the river meets the sand and sea". "You were perfect for me."

"These miraculous signs will accompany those who believe: They will cast out demons in my name, and they will speak in new languages" Mark 16:17 NLT

December 23rd, 2018

I want to feel your arms around me telling me it's going to be okay. I know it is. I've done well this past year and I know the next one will be better.

"He will once again fill your mouth with laughter and your lips with shouts of joy."
Job 8:21 NLT

December 28th, 2018

I am so thankful for my faith and my ability to see the joy in the pain, to experience miracles and not fear. I know my faith is what has gotten me through these past twelve months. I know, trust and believe God has a plan and our lives are already determined by Him. The length of our time on Earth has been set. We need to live everyday being the best version of ourselves, as holy as possible. Without God is the center of our life we turn to anger and fear. With God we don't have to be afraid, we can be still and see the peace and joy in our lives. I really have found that I need to take time to listen to hear what God wants me to know. His word is also a huge comfort to me. To see all the people that experienced healing and witnessed miracles when they believed in God and not in the world.

"While he was still speaking, a bright cloud covered them, and a voice from the cloud said, "This is my Son, whom I love; with him I am well pleased. Listen to him!""
Matthew 17:5 NIV

I choose joy. Joy in myself, Joy during grief. Joy in my boys, my family, my friends. Joy my job. Joy my memories. Joy in all that I do. Joy starts with gratitude.

"For I have given rest to the weary and joy to the sorrowing." Jeremiah 31:25 NLT

I don't have to be the same as I was before. I can't be the same as I was before because it's not the same as it was before. And that's okay.

"Whatever is good and perfect comes down to us from God our Father, who created all the lights in the heavens. He never changes or casts a shifting shadow."
James 1:17 NLT

December 19, 2019

2 Years

I needed the Joy I found this year. I am so glad for my faith and trust in God. I don't know how people without faith begin to get through something like this because it is hard even with faith. It is not always easy to trust in God's plan, but I also don't feel like I have a choice.

I am proud of who I am becoming. I feel stronger. I feel okay most days. I feel that the boys are learning to cope without you here. School is still hard for both of them and I think Michael is struggling too. Winter, the anniversary, hunting season and holidays all affect us right now.

In some ways the two years have gone by very fast and other times I feel like you have been gone for so long. I still miss you. I still wish you could be here to help with parenting especially.

I worry if it's okay to be okay. I wonder if others are okay too? I know there is not a rule book and there never will be, but I sure wish someone offered guidance on how to do this. It is so different for every person and no two people or families are alike. God does know what is best for us and we just have to believe that this is where we are meant to be. We need to trust that God will continue to bless us daily with miracles and guidance. He will never forsake us or leave us to do this alone.

My word for 2020 is going to be confidence. Confidence in God's plan and His love for me. Confidence in myself. Confidence in my parenting skills. Confidence in my self-image. Confidence to make decisions and set boundaries. I feel that the last three years, strength, peace and joy were very appropriate, and God has guided me with each of those things.

Dear God,

Thank you for the memories, the time we did have, the strength you provide and the constant love you have for all of us. I thank you most for the promise of heaven. Thank you for your Son our Lord Jesus Christ and his sacrifice for us. Thank you for scripture to guide me in my daily life to become the best version of myself and to live as you intended for me. Thank you for having confidence in me to be a widow and single parent, to take on a new job and to learn new things. Amen.

"On that day they will say, "Surely this is our God; we trusted in him, and he saved us. his is the Lord, we trusted in him; let us rejoice and be glad in his salvation."
Isaiah 25:9 NIV

Acknowledgements

Thank you to Jen Davis for her encouragement to write my story. Your love and support were crucial during those first few months.

Thank you to my talented cousin Lisa of Lisa Marie Anderson Photography for the amazing photo shoot.

Thank you to Cathleen, Lisa, and Jayne for the counseling, love, healing and friendship. Thank you to Diane and Emily for always listening during my massage or myofascial release appointments.

Thank you to all that helped with editing, the not so fun part of the writing process.

Thank you to Hope*Writers from all the information and inspiration about publishing. Without your guidance, this would not be a reality.

A HUGE thank you to my family and friends for the continued love and support as we all go on this journey together and yet in our own ways. I love you all!

And most importantly to Steve, for loving me, supporting me, having confidence in my abilities and for continuing to watch over us. Thank you for encouraging us all to live our faith and to support others. I love you! (And of course, Amazing Grace just started playing on the meditation station as I typed this paragraph.)

Made in the USA
Monee, IL
28 March 2020

24062395R00088